a
simple
daily
prayer

D1550772

a
simple
daily
prayer

a pattern of prayer for
morning and evening
for individuals or
small groups

Father
Andrew
Moore

kevin
mayhew

First published in 1998.
This edition published in 2003 by

KEVIN MAYHEW LTD
Buxhall, Stowmarket, Suffolk IP14 3BW
E-mail: info@kevinmayhewltd.com

KINGSGATE PUBLISHING INC
1000 Pannell Street, Suite G, Columbia, MO 65201
E-mail: sales@kingsgatepublishing.com

9 8 7 6 5 4 3 2 1 0

ISBN 1 84417 168 X
Catalogue No 1500654

Cover design by Angela Selfe
Printed and bound in Great Britain

CONTENTS

ACKNOWLEDGEMENTS

The publishers wish to express their gratitude to the following for permission to include copyright material in this book:

Darton Longman & Todd Ltd, 1 Spencer Court, 140-142 Wandsworth High Street, London, SW18 4JJ for the Bible quotations which are taken from the *New Jerusalem Bible*, published and copyright 1985 Darton, Longman and Todd Ltd and les Editions du Cerf, and used by permission of the publishers.

A. P. Watt Ltd, Literary Agents, 20 John Street, London, WC1N 2DR on behalf of The Grail, England for the Psalms which are taken from *The Psalms: A New Translation*. Also on behalf of the Liturgy Commission for the prayers for morning and evening which are taken from the *Divine Office*.

Every effort has been made to trace the owners of copyright material and we hope that no copyright has been infringed. Pardon is sought and apology made if the contrary be the case and a correction will be made in any reprint of this book.

INTRODUCTION

Increasingly, many people are discovering the benefits of joining with the Church in its daily prayer as an enrichment to their own prayer life. The Prayer of the Church, with its Office of Readings, Morning, Midday, Evening and Night Prayer, is said daily by Priests, Religious and many others throughout the world.

Those who are attracted to saying the complete Divine Office, or even the simpler form of Morning and Evening Prayer, may be dissuaded by the need for some familiarity with liturgy and the Church Calendar of Seasons and Saints, as well as for a good deal of time. The necessity of having to purchase the set of three volumes required for the complete English version of the Divine Office may also deter those who are unfamiliar with this form of prayer, or who are uncertain of their ability to commit the necessary time.

A Simple Daily Prayer offers an introduction to the structure and content of the Divine Office for those whose lives may be busy but who, nevertheless, wish to enrich their prayer life.

For each day of a monthly cycle a Morning and Evening Prayer is provided. The format given for each day may be used either in its entirety or in part, depending on circumstances. The traditional Night Prayer (Compline) is also provided.

Each Office begins with an introductory verse and 'Glory be'. A psalm, or part of a psalm, appropriate to the time of day is then said. The Book of Psalms is a source of a rich variety of spiritual sentiment and prayer. To newcomers it may come as a surprise to find sentiments of anger and loathing in prayer set alongside repentance, praise and joy. But the Psalms bring the whole of human life into the spiritual arena, so that the Spirit may enter the whole of human life. After the Psalm there is a short reading taken from Holy Scripture.

The Gospel canticles (the Benedictus and the Magnificat) are an essential part of the Prayer of the Church and are sung, or said, every day. The Benedictus is said at Morning Prayer. It is the hymn of praise spoken by Zechariah at the birth and naming of his son, John the Baptist. It is sung at the beginning of each day to welcome the new light of Christ foretold by John the Baptist. The Magnificat, sung at Evening Prayer, is the response of Our Lady to the Incarnation, the response of her soul to the dignity granted her in becoming the Mother of God. For each of these canticles an antiphon is given, taken from the Gospels. The same antiphon is used at both Morning and Evening Prayer, to remind us that the canticles are themselves from the Gospel, and to give us a phrase from the Gospel to meditate on throughout the day. The antiphon is said before and after the Benedictus or Magnificat.

There are three prayers of intercession, to which other personal intercessions may be added. After the recitation of the 'Our Father', there is a concluding prayer which is taken from the complete Divine Office. Each Office ends with the verse of blessing and thanksgiving.

A Simple Daily Prayer may be said alone or by several people praying together. The plural 'we' and 'our' is used throughout and although, when using the book alone, the singular 'I' could be substituted, it is perhaps more helpful to use the plural to remind us that in this prayer we are uniting ourselves in the Holy Spirit with countless others throughout the world who are also at prayer in the name of Jesus Christ, to the greater glory and praise of God the Father.

ANDREW MOORE

GOSPEL CANTICLES

The Benedictus (Luke 1: 68-79)

Blessed be the Lord, the God of Israel!
He has visited his people and redeemed them.

He has raised up for us a mighty saviour
in the house of David his servant,
as he promised by the lips of holy men,
those who were his prophets from of old.

A saviour who would free us from our foes,
from the hands of all who hate us.
So his love for our fathers is fulfilled
and his holy covenant remembered.

He swore to Abraham our father to grant us,
that free from fear, and saved from the hands of our foes,
we might serve him in holiness and justice
all the days of our life in his presence.

As for you, little child,
you shall be called a prophet of God, the Most High.
You shall go ahead of the Lord
to prepare his ways before him,

To make known to his people their salvation
through forgiveness of all their sins,
the loving-kindness of the heart of our God
who visits us like the dawn from on high.

He will give light to those in darkness,
those who dwell in the shadow of death,
and guide us into the way of peace.

Glory be to the Father, and to the Son, and to the Holy Spirit.
As it was in the beginning, is now and ever shall be,
world without end. Amen

The Magnificat (Luke 1:46-55)

My soul glorifies the Lord,
my spirit rejoices in God, my Saviour.
He looks on his servant in her lowliness;
henceforth all ages will call me blessed.

The Almighty works marvels for me.
Holy his name!
His mercy is from age to age,
on those who fear him.

He puts forth his arm in strength
and scatters the proud-hearted.
He casts the mighty from their thrones
and raises the lowly.

He fills the starving with good things,
sends the rich away empty.

He protects Israel, his servant,
remembering his mercy,
the mercy promised to our fathers,
to Abraham and his sons for ever.

Glory be . . .

O Lord, open our lips,
and our mouth shall proclaim your praise.
Glory be to the Father, and to the Son, and to the Holy Spirit.
As it was in the beginning, is now and ever shall be,
world without end. Amen.

Psalm 8

How great is your name, O Lord our God,
through all the earth!

Your majesty is praised above the heavens;
on the lips of children and of babes
you have found praise to foil your enemy,
to silence the foe and the rebel.

When I see the heavens, the work of your hands,
the moon and the stars which you arranged,
what are we that you should keep us in mind,
mere mortals that you care for us?

Yet you have made us little less than gods;
and crowned us with glory and honour,
you gave us power over the work of your hands,
put all things under our feet.

All of them, sheep and cattle,
yes, even the savage beasts,

birds of the air, and fish
that make their way through the waters.

How great is your name, O Lord our God,
through all the earth!

Glory be . . .

Reading Romans 11:33-36

How rich and deep are the wisdom and the knowledge of God! We cannot reach to the root of his decisions or his ways. Who has ever known the mind of the Lord? Who has ever been his adviser? Who has given anything to him, so that his presents come only as a debt returned? Everything there is comes from him and is caused by him and exists for him. To him be glory for ever! Amen.

Canticle with Gospel antiphon

In the beginning was the Word; the Word was with God and the Word was God. (John 1:1)

Benedictus (p. 10)

Intercessions

Lord of all creation,
we thank you for the gift of this new day;
fill it with your love.
– Come, Lord Jesus,

May your love guide and protect us during this day,
that we may work for your glory
and for our neighbour's good.
– Come, Lord Jesus.

Bless your Church, Lord,
as she strives to bear witness to the Good News.
– Come, Lord Jesus.

(Personal intercessions may be added here.)

Our Father . . .

Prayer

Lord, be the beginning and end
of all that we do and say.
Prompt our actions with your grace,
and complete them with your all-powerful help.
We make our prayer through Christ our Lord. Amen.
(Morning Prayer, Monday, Week 1)

Let us bless the Lord.
Thanks be to God.

Evening Prayer

O God, come to our aid.
O Lord, make haste to help us.
Glory be . . .

Psalm 141 (142)

With all my voice I cry to you, Lord,
with all my voice I entreat you, Lord.
I pour out my trouble before you;
I tell you all my distress
while my spirit faints within me.
But you, O Lord, know my path.

On the way where I shall walk
they have hidden a snare to entrap me.
Look on my right and see:
there is no one who takes my part.
I have no means of escape,
not one who cares for my soul.

I cry to you, O Lord.
I have said: 'You are my refuge,
all I have in the land of the living.'
Listen, then, to my cry
for I am in the depths of distress.

Rescue me from those who pursue me
for they are stronger than I.
Bring my soul out of this prison

and then I shall praise your name.
Around me the just will assemble
because of your goodness to me.

Glory be . . .

Reading 1 Corinthians 2:7-10

It is of the mysterious wisdom of God that we talk, the
wisdom that was hidden, which God predestined to be for
our glory before the ages began. None of the rulers of the
age recognised it; for if they had recognised it, they would
not have crucified the Lord of glory; but it is as scripture
says: 'What no eye has seen and no ear has heard, what
the mind of man cannot visualise; all that God has
prepared for those who love him'. To us, though, God has
given revelation through the Spirit, for the Spirit explores
the depths of everything, even the depths of God.

Canticle with Gospel antiphon

In the beginning was the Word; the Word was with God
and the Word was God. (John 1:1)

Magnificat (p. 11)

Intercessions

Bless your Church, Lord,
that the world may see in her
the goodness of your love.
– Lord, give us your peace.

Inspire within us mutual understanding and respect;
enable us to rejoice
in the richness and diversity of human character.
– Lord, give us your peace.

Be with those who are lonely this evening
and comfort those who are afraid.
– Lord, give us your peace.

(Personal intercessions may be added here.)

Our Father . . .

Prayer

Let our worship give you glory, Lord,
who for our salvation looked upon
the lowliness of Mary your handmaid:
raise us up to share with her
the fulness of redemption.
We make our prayer through Christ our Lord. Amen.
(Evening Prayer, Monday, Week 1)

Let us bless the Lord.
Thanks be to God.

O Lord, open our lips,
and our mouth shall proclaim your praise.
Glory be . . .

Psalm 5:1-9

To my words give ear, O Lord,
give ear to my groaning.
Attend to the sound of my cries,
my King and my God.

It is you whom I invoke, O Lord.
In the morning you hear me;
in the morning I offer you my prayer,
watching and waiting.

You are no God who loves evil;
no sinner is your guest.
The boastful shall not stand their ground
before your face.

You hate all who do evil;
you destroy all who lie.
Deceitful and bloodthirsty people
are hateful to you, Lord.

But I through the greatness of your love
have access to your house.
I bow down before your holy temple,
filled with awe.

Lead me, Lord, in your justice,
because of those who lie in wait;
make clear your way before me.

Glory be . . .

Reading 1 Peter 1:13-16

Your minds, then, must be sober and ready for action; put all your hope in the grace brought to you by the revelation of Jesus Christ. Do not allow yourselves to be shaped by the passions of your old ignorance, but as obedient children, be yourselves holy in all your activity, after the model of the Holy One who calls us, since scripture says, 'Be holy, for I am holy'.

Canticle with Gospel antiphon

Anyone who does the will of God, that person is my brother and sister and mother. (Mark 3:35)

Benedictus (p. 10)

Intercessions

May your name be held holy
in all that we do today.
– Be with us, Lord, this day.

May those who work to build our society
be moved to work creatively
with your Spirit.
– Be with us, Lord, this day.

May those who are unable to work,
or cannot find work,
be strengthened in their spirit and self-regard.
– Be with us, Lord, this day.

(Personal intercessions may be added here.)

Our Father . . .

Prayer

Look with favour on our morning prayer, Lord,
and in your saving love
let your light penetrate the hidden places of our hearts.
May no sordid desires darken our minds,
renewed and enlightened as we are by your heavenly grace.
We make our prayer through Christ our Lord. Amen.
(Morning Prayer, Tuesday, Week 1)

Let us bless the Lord.
Thanks be to God.

O God, come to our aid.
O Lord, make haste to help us.
Glory be . . .

Psalm 15 (16)

Preserve me, God, I take refuge in you.
I say to the Lord: 'You are my God.
My happiness lies in you alone.'

You have put into my heart a marvellous love
for the faithful ones who dwell in your land.
Those who choose other gods increase their sorrows.
Never will I offer their offerings of blood.
Never will I take their name upon my lips.

O Lord, it is you who are my portion and cup,
it is you yourself who are my prize.
The lot marked out for me is my delight,
welcome indeed the heritage that falls to me!

I will bless you, Lord, you give me counsel,
and even at night direct my heart.
I keep you, Lord, ever in my sight;
since you are at my right hand, I shall stand firm.

And so my heart rejoices, my soul is glad;
even my body shall rest in safety.
For you will not leave my soul among the dead,
nor let your beloved know decay.

You will show me the path of life,
the fullness of joy in your presence,
at your right hand happiness for ever.

Glory be . . .

Reading 1 John 4:7-11

My dear friends, let us love one another, since love is from God and everyone who loves is a child of God and knows God. Whoever fails to love does not know God, because God is love. This is the revelation of God's love for us, that God sent his only Son into the world that we might have life through him. Love consists in this: it is not we who loved God, but God loved us and sent his Son to expiate our sins. My dear friends, if God loved us so much, we too should love one another.

Canticle with Gospel antiphon

Anyone who does the will of God, that person is my brother and sister and mother. (Mark 3:35)

Magnificat (p. 11)

Intercessions

We pray for justice in the world,
that all people may come
to live in your peace.
– Lord, hear our prayer.

Have mercy on those who have lost their lives
in violence and tragedy;
take them into your peace.
– Lord, hear our prayer.

May those who provide us
with entertainment and relaxation
always be mindful of the dignity of human life.
– Lord, hear our prayer.

(Personal intercessions may be added here.)

Our Father . . .

Prayer

We give you thanks, Lord God Almighty,
for bringing us safely to the evening of this day;
we humbly ask that the prayer we make with uplifted hands
may be an offering pleasing in your sight.
We make this prayer through Christ our Lord. Amen.
                    (Evening Prayer, Tuesday, Week 1)

Let us bless the Lord.
Thanks be to God.

O Lord, open our lips,
and our mouth shall proclaim your praise.
Glory be . . .

Psalm 9:2-11

I will praise you, Lord, with all my heart;
I will recount all your wonders.
I will rejoice in you and be glad,
and sing psalms to your name, O Most High.

See how my enemies turn back,
how they stumble and perish before you.
You upheld the justice of my cause;
you sat enthroned, judging with justice.

You have checked the nations, destroyed the wicked;
you have wiped out their name for ever and ever.
The foe is destroyed, eternally ruined.
You uprooted their cities; their memory has perished.

But the Lord sits enthroned for ever.
The throne is set up for judgement.
God will judge the world with justice,
and will judge the peoples with truth.

For the oppressed let the Lord be a stronghold,
a stronghold in times of distress.
Those who know your name will trust you;
you will never forsake those who seek you.

Glory be . . .

Reading 2 Corinthians 5:1-5

For we are well aware that when the tent that houses us on earth is folded up, there is a house for us from God, not made by human hands but everlasting, in the heavens. And in this earthly state we do indeed groan, longing to put on our heavenly home over the present one; if indeed we are to be found clothed rather than stripped bare. Yes, indeed, in this present tent, we groan under the burden, not that we want to be stripped of our covering, but because we want to be covered with a second garment on top, so that what is mortal in us may be swallowed up by life. It is God who designed us for this very purpose, and he has given us the Spirit as a pledge.

Canticle with Gospel antiphon

I must proclaim the Good News of the kingdom of God, because that is what I was sent to do. (Luke 4:43)

Benedictus (p. 10)

Intercessions

As we start a new day and ask your blessing,
we pray for your special blessing
on those who are born into this world today.
– Lord Jesus, you are our strength.

May we come to see you in others,
especially in those who are rejected by society,
or by themselves.
– Lord Jesus, you are our strength.

Be with us, Lord,
as we face the demands
and the temptations of this day.
– Lord Jesus, you are our strength.

(Personal intercessions may be added here.)

Our Father . . .

Prayer

God our Saviour.
through the grace of baptism
you made us children of light.
Hear our prayer that we may always walk in that light
and work for truth as your witnesses.
We make this prayer through Christ our Lord. Amen.
(Morning Prayer, Wednesday, Week 1)

Let us bless the Lord.
Thanks be to God.

O God, come to our aid.
O Lord, make haste to help us.
Glory be . . .

Psalm 16 (17):1-9, 14b-15

Lord, hear a cause that is just,
pay heed to my cry.
Turn your ear to my prayer,
no deceit is on my lips.

From you may my judgement come forth.
Your eyes discern the truth.

You search my heart, you visit me by night.
You test me and you find in me no wrong.
My words are not sinful like human words.

I kept from violence because of your word,
I kept my feet firmly in your paths;
there was no faltering in my steps.

I am here and I call, you will hear me, O God.
Turn your ear to me; hear my words.
Display your great love, you whose right hand saves
your friends from those who rebel against them.

Guard me as the apple of your eye.
Hide me in the shadow of your wings
from the violent attack of the wicked.

You give them their fill of your treasures;
they rejoice in abundance of offspring
and leave their wealth to their children.

As for me, in my justice I shall see your face
and be filled, when I awake, with the sight of your glory.

Glory be . . .

Reading 1 John 3:1-2

You must see what great love the Father has lavished on us by letting us be called God's children – which is what we are! The reason why the world does not acknowledge us is that it did not acknowledge him. My dear friends, we are already God's children, but what we shall be in the future has not yet been revealed. We are well aware that when he appears we shall be like him, because we shall see him as he really is.

Canticle with Gospel antiphon

I must proclaim the Good News of the kingdom of God, because that is what I was sent to do. (Luke 4:43)

Magnificat (p. 11)

Intercessions

Guide those who serve us in leadership in Church and state;
may they be wise in their thoughts
and just in their decisions.
– Lord, have mercy.

Bless our families, our friends and colleagues:
may your love be with them tonight.
– Christ, have mercy.

Lord, be with those who are dying;
comfort them with your love.
– Lord, have mercy.

(Personal intercessions may be added here.)

Our Father . . .

Prayer

Lord, support us as we pray,
protect us day and night,
so that we who under your guiding hand
live in a world of change,
may always draw strength from you,
with whom there is no shadow of alteration.
We make our prayer through Christ our Lord. Amen.
                    (Evening Prayer, Wednesday, Week 1)

Let us bless the Lord.
Thanks be to God.

Morning Prayer

O Lord, open our lips,
and our mouth shall proclaim your praise.
Glory be . . .

Psalm 9:12-21

Sing psalms to the Lord who dwells in Zion.
Proclaim God's mighty works among the peoples,
for the Avenger of blood has remembered them,
has not forgotten the cry of the poor.

Have pity on me, Lord, see my sufferings,
you who save me from the gates of death;
that I may recount all your praise
at the gates of the city of Zion
and rejoice in your saving help.

The nations have fallen in the pit which they have made,
their feet caught in the snare they laid.
The Lord is revealed, has given judgement.
The wicked are snared in the work of their own hands.

Let the wicked go down among the dead,
all the nations forgetful of God;
for the needy shall not always be forgotten
nor the hopes of the poor be in vain.

Arise, Lord, let mortals not prevail!
Let the nations be judged before you.
Lord, strike them with terror,
let the nations know they are but mortals.

Glory be . . .

Reading 1 Corinthians 12:4-6

There are many different gifts, but it is always the same
Spirit; there are many different ways of serving, but it is
always the same Lord. There are many different forms of
activity, but in everybody it is the same God who is at
work in them all.

Canticle with Gospel antiphon

Come to me, all you who labour and are overburdened,
and I will give you rest. (Matthew 11:28)

Benedictus (p. 10)

Intercessions

Through the Spirit, Lord, you give us many gifts;
may we use those gifts wisely today.
– Come, Holy Spirit.

Christ came to forgive sins;
help us to forgive others as you forgive us.
– Come, Holy Spirit.

Help us to see what needs to be done
and to have the courage to do it.
– Come, Holy Spirit.

(Personal intercessions may be added here.)

Our Father . . .

Prayer

Almighty ever-living God,
we make our prayer to you at morning, noon and evening:
dispel from our hearts the darkness of sin,
and bring us to the true light, Christ your Son,
who lives and reigns with you and the Holy Spirit,
God, for ever and ever. Amen.

(Morning Prayer, Thursday, Week 1)

Let us bless the Lord.
Thanks be to God.

O God, come to our aid.
O Lord, make haste to help us.
Glory be . . .

Psalm 25 (26)

Give judgement for me, O Lord,
for I walk the path of perfection.
I trust in the Lord; I have not wavered.

Examine me, Lord, and try me;
O test my heart and my mind,
for your love is before my eyes
and I walk according to your truth.

I never take my place with liars
and with hypocrites I shall not go.
I hate the evildoer's company;
I will not take my place with the wicked.

To prove my innocence I wash my hands
and take my place around your altar,
singing a song of thanksgiving,
proclaiming all your wonders.

O Lord, I love the house where you dwell,
the place where your glory abides.

Do not sweep me away with sinners,
nor my life with bloodthirsty people
in whose hands are evil plots,
whose right hands are filled with gold.

As for me, I walk the path of perfection.
Redeem me and show me your mercy.
My foot stands on level ground;
I will bless the Lord in the assembly.

Glory be . . .

Reading Romans 6:8-11

We believe that, if we died with Christ, then we shall live
with him too. We know that Christ has been raised from
the dead and will never die again. Death has no power
over him any more. For by dying, he is dead to sin once
and for all, and now the life that he lives is life with God.
In the same way, you must see yourselves as being dead
to sin but alive for God in Christ Jesus.

Canticle with Gospel antiphon

Come to me, all you who labour and are overburdened,
and I will give you rest. (Matthew 11:28)

Magnificat (p. 11)

Intercessions

We thank you for the gift of faith;
help those who have no faith, or whose faith is troubled.
– Come, Lord Jesus, give us your peace.

We pray for those who work this evening
in caring for others.
– Come, Lord Jesus, come in peace.

We pray for those who have no home to go to tonight;
ease their loneliness and give them hope.
– Come, Lord Jesus, come in peace.

(Personal intercessions may be added here.)

Our Father . . .

Prayer

Lord God,
you give the moon to illumine the night,
and to dispel the darkness you bring in the light of day:
grant that during this night
we may elude the grasp of Satan
and in the morning rise to give you praise.
We make this prayer through Christ our Lord. Amen.

(Evening Prayer, Thursday, Week 1)

Let us bless the Lord.
Thanks be to God.

O Lord, open our lips,
and our mouth shall proclaim your praise.
Glory be . . .

Psalm 46 (47)

All peoples, clap your hands,
cry to God with shouts of joy!
For the Lord, the Most High, we must fear,
great king over all the earth.

God subdues peoples under us
and nations under our feet.
Our inheritance, our glory, is from God,
given to Jacob out of love.

God goes up with shouts of joy;
the Lord goes up with trumpet blast.
Sing praise for God, sing praise,
sing praise to our king, sing praise.

God is king of all the earth,
sing praise with all your skill.
God is king over the nations;
God reigns enthroned in holiness.

The leaders of the people are assembled
with the people of Abraham's God.
The rulers of the earth belong to God,
to God who reigns over all.

Glory be . . .

Reading Wisdom 7:15-16

May God grant me to speak as he would wish and conceive thoughts worthy of the gifts I have received, since he is both guide to wisdom and director of sages; for we are in his hand, yes, ourselves and our sayings, and all intellectual and all practical knowledge.

Canticle with Gospel antiphon

And a voice came from heaven, 'You are my Son, the Beloved; my favour rests on you'. (Mark 1:11)

Benedictus (p. 10)

Intercessions

Lord, with the dawning of a new day
we celebrate our faith in the Resurrection;
may it give us hope.
– Lord, bless your people.

Be with those who have unpleasant tasks to do today
and with those who are anxious about their work.
– Lord, bless your people.

Be with those who are suffering today in mind or body.
– Lord, bless your people.

(Personal intercessions may be added here.)

Our Father . . .

Prayer

Lord God,
you hold out the light of your Word
to those who do not know you.
Strengthen in our hearts the faith you have given us,
so that no trials may quench the fire
your Spirit has kindled within us.
We make this prayer through Christ our Lord. Amen.
(Morning Prayer, Friday, Week 1)

Let us bless the Lord.
Thanks be to God.

O God, come to our aid.
O Lord, make haste to help us.
Glory be . . .

Psalm 62 (63):1-9

O God, you are my God, for you I long;
for you my soul is thirsting.
My body pines for you
like a dry, weary land without water.
So I gaze on you in the sanctuary
to see your strength and your glory.

For your love is better than life,
my lips will speak your praise.
So will I bless you all my life,
in your name I will lift up my hands.
My soul shall be filled as with a banquet,
my mouth shall praise you with joy.

On my bed I remember you.
On you I muse through the night
for you have been my help;
in the shadow of your wings I rejoice.
My soul clings to you;
your right hand holds me fast.

Glory be

Reading Ephesians 4:29-32

No foul word should ever cross your lips; let your words be for the improvement of others, as occasion offers, and do good to your listeners; do not grieve the Holy Spirit of God who has marked you with his seal, ready for the day when we shall be set free. Any bitterness or bad temper or anger or shouting or abuse must be far removed from you – as must every kind of malice. Be generous to one another, sympathetic, forgiving each other as readily as God forgave you in Christ.

Canticle with Gospel antiphon

And a voice came from heaven, 'You are my Son, the Beloved; my favour rests on you'. (Mark 1:11)

Magnificat (p. 11)

Intercessions

Comfort those who are lonely tonight,
those who are abandoned
and those in despair.
– Be with us, Lord, this night.

As we sleep this night,
others will be working for our benefit;
sustain them in their labour.
– Be with us, Lord, this night.

Strengthen our faith,
that we may be faithful
in hearing and living your Word.
– Be with us, Lord, this night.

(Personal intercessions may be added here.)

Our Father . . .

Prayer

Lord God,
teach us the lessons of your Son's Passion,
and so enable us, your people,
to bear the yoke he makes light for us.
We make this prayer through Christ our Lord. Amen.
(Evening Prayer, Friday, Week 1)

Let us bless the Lord.
Thanks be to God.

O Lord, open our lips,
and our mouth shall proclaim your praise.
Glory be . . .

Psalm 92 (93)

The Lord is king, with majesty enrobed;
the Lord is robed with might,
and girded round with power.

The world you made firm, not to be moved;
your throne has stood firm from of old.
From all eternity, O Lord, you are.

The waters have lifted up, O Lord,
the waters have lifted up their voice.
the waters have lifted up their thunder.

Greater than the roar of mighty waters,
more glorious than the surgings of the sea,
the Lord is glorious on high.

Truly your decrees are to be trusted.
Holiness is fitting to your house,
O Lord, until the end of time.

Glory be . . .

Reading Romans 14:17-19

It is not eating and drinking that make the kingdom of God, but the saving justice, the peace and the joy brought by the Holy Spirit. It is the person who serves Christ in these things that will be approved by God and respected by everyone. So then, let us be always seeking the ways which lead to peace and the ways in which we can support one another.

Canticle with Gospel antiphon

Let anyone who is thirsty come to me! Let anyone who believes in me come and drink. (John 7:37b-38)

Benedictus (p. 10)

Intercessions

Lord, may we come to be more aware
of your presence among us
and to respect, in love, the creation you have given us.
– Lord, open our hearts to your love.

Christ is the Light of the world;
may that light be our guide
through the dark moments of the day.
– Lord, open our hearts to your love.

Lord, may we be generous of heart
to those we meet today.
– Lord, open our hearts to your love.

(Personal intercessions may be added here.)

Our Father . . .

Prayer

Let the splendour of the resurrection,
light up our hearts and minds, Lord,
scattering the shadows of death,
and bringing us to the radiance of eternity.
We make this prayer through Christ our Lord. Amen.
(Morning Prayer, Saturday, Week 1)

Let us bless the Lord.
Thanks be to God.

O God, come to our aid.
O Lord, make haste to help us.
Glory be . . .

Psalm 111 (112)

Happy are those who fear the Lord,
who take delight in all God's commands.
Their descendants shall be powerful on earth;
the children of the upright are blessed.

Wealth and riches are in their homes;
their justice stands firm for ever.
They are lights in the darkness for the upright;
they are generous, merciful and just.

Good people take pity and lend,
they conduct their affairs with honour.
The just will never waver,
they will be remembered for ever.

They have no fear of evil news;
with firm hearts they trust in the Lord.
With steadfast hearts they will not fear;
they will see the downfall of their foes.

Openhanded, they give to the poor;
their justice stands firm for ever.
Their heads will be raised in glory.

The wicked shall see this and be angry,
shall grind their teeth and pine away;
the desires of the wicked lead to doom.

Glory be . . .

Reading Ephesians 1:3-10

Blessed be God the Father of our Lord Jesus Christ, who
has blessed us with all the spiritual blessings of heaven in
Christ. Thus he chose us in Christ before the world was
made to be holy and faultless before him in love, marking
us out for himself beforehand, to be adopted sons and
daughters, through Jesus Christ. Such was his purpose
and good pleasure, to the praise of the glory of his grace,
his free gift to us in the Beloved, in whom, through his
blood, we gain our freedom, the forgiveness of our sins.
Such is the richness of the grace which he has showered
on us in all wisdom and insight. He has let us know the
mystery of his purpose, according to his good pleasure
which he determined beforehand in Christ, for him to act
upon when the times had run their course: that he would
bring everything together under Christ, as head, everything in the heavens and everything on earth.

Canticle with Gospel antiphon

Let anyone who is thirsty come to me! Let anyone who
believes in me come and drink. (John 7:37b-38)

Magnificat (p. 11)

Intercessions

Keep your Church faithful in proclaiming
your message of forgiveness, hope and love.
– Lord Jesus, you are our peace.

Comfort and strengthen those
who have received sad or troubling news today.
– Lord Jesus, you are our peace.

Be with all those throughout the world
who are united this evening in praying in Christ's name.
– Lord Jesus, you are our peace.

(Personal intercessions may be added here.)

Our Father . . .

Prayer

Lord God,
living light of eternal love,
grant that always aglow with charity,
we may love you above all else
and our sisters and brothers for your sake,
with one and the selfsame love.
We make this prayer through Christ our Lord. Amen.

(Midday Prayer, Saturday, Week 1)

Let us bless the Lord.
Thanks be to God.

O Lord, open our lips,
and our mouth shall proclaim your praise.
Glory be . . .

Psalm 66 (67)

O God, be gracious and bless us
and let your face shed its light upon us.
So will your ways be known upon earth
and all nations learn your saving help.

Let the peoples praise you, O God;
let all the peoples praise you.

Let the nations be glad and exult
for you rule the world with justice.
With fairness you rule the peoples,
you guide the nations on earth.

The earth has yielded its fruit
for God, our God, has blessed us.
May God still give us blessing
till the ends of the earth stand in awe.

Let the peoples praise you, O God;
let all the peoples praise you.

Glory be . . .

Reading Hebrews 13:20-21

I pray that the God of peace, who brought back from the dead our Lord Jesus, the great Shepherd of the sheep, by the blood that sealed an eternal covenant, may prepare you to do his will in every kind of good action; effecting in us all whatever is acceptable to himself through Jesus Christ, to whom be glory for ever and ever, Amen.

Canticle with Gospel antiphon

Jesus said, 'It is not those who are well who need the doctor, but the sick. I have come to call not the upright but sinners to repentance'. (Luke 5:31, 32)

Benedictus (p. 10)

Intercessions

You have renewed us in baptism;
renew us again today in your love.
– Lord, we trust in you.

Strengthen those, Lord,
who are in need of our prayers this morning,
especially those unable to care for themselves.
– Lord, we trust in you.

May we bring joy and hope,
not sorrow or pain,

to those we meet today.
– Lord, we trust in you.

(Personal intercessions may be added here.)

Our Father . . .

Prayer

Almighty Lord and God,
protect us by your power throughout the course of this day,
even as you have enabled us to begin it:
do not let us turn aside to any sin,
but let our every thought, word and deed
aim at doing what is pleasing in your sight.
We make this prayer through Christ our Lord. Amen.

(Morning Prayer, Monday, Week 2)

Let us bless the Lord.
Thanks be to God.

O God, come to our aid.
O Lord, make haste to help us.
Glory be . . .

Psalm 40 (41)

Happy those who consider the poor and the weak.
The Lord will save them in the evil day,
will guard them, give them life, make them happy in
    the land
and will not give them up to the will of their foes.
The Lord will give them strength in their pain,
will bring them back from sickness to health.

As for me, I said: 'Lord, have mercy on me,
heal my soul for I have sinned against you.'
My foes are speaking evil against me.
They want me to die and my name to perish.
They come to visit me and speak empty words,
their hearts full of malice, they spread it abroad.

My enemies whisper together against me.
They all weigh up the evil which is upon me.
They say something deadly is fixed upon me
and I will not rise from where I lie.
Thus even my friend, in whom I trusted,
who ate my bread, has turned against me.

But you, O Lord, have mercy on me.
Let me rise once more and I will repay them.
By this I shall know that you are my friend,
if my foes do not shout in triumph over me.
If you uphold me I shall be unharmed
and set in your presence for evermore.

Glory be . . .

Reading 1 Peter 4:13-14

In so far as you share in the sufferings of Christ, be glad, so that you may enjoy a much greater gladness when his glory is revealed. If you are insulted for bearing Christ's name, blessed are you, for on you rests the Spirit of God, the Spirit of glory.

Canticle with Gospel antiphon

Jesus said, 'It is not those who are well who need the doctor, but the sick. I have come to call not the upright but sinners to repentance'. (Luke 5:31, 32)

Magnificat (p. 11)

Intercessions

We pray for Christian families;
may they be strengthened in their witness of faith.
– Bless your people, Lord.

We give thanks for the nourishment you give us
and pray for the relief of hunger and poverty.
– Bless your people, Lord.

Give rest to those who have died today;
welcome them into your peace.
– Bless your people, Lord.

(Personal intercessions may be added here.)

Our Father . . .

Prayer

All-powerful God,
since you have given us, your unworthy servants,
the strength to work throughout this day:
accept this evening sacrifice of praise
as we thank you for your gifts.
We make this prayer through Christ our Lord. Amen.

(Evening Prayer, Monday, Week 2)

Let us bless the Lord.
Thanks be to God.

O Lord, open our lips,
and our mouth shall proclaim your praise.
Glory be . . .

Psalm 1

Happy indeed are those
who follow not the counsel of the wicked,
nor linger in the way of sinners
nor sit in the company of scorners,
but whose delight is the law of the Lord
and who ponder God's law day and night.

They are like a tree that is planted
beside the flowing waters,
that yields its fruit in due season
and whose leaves shall never fade;
and all that they do shall prosper.
Not so are the wicked, not so!

For they like winnowed chaff
shall be driven away by the wind.
When the wicked are judged they shall not stand,
nor find room among those who are just;
for the Lord guards the way of the just
but the way of the wicked leads to doom.

Glory be . . .

Reading James 1:2-4

Consider it a great joy when trials of many kinds come upon you, for you well know that the testing of your faith produces perseverance, and perseverance must complete its work so that you will become fully developed, complete, not deficient in any way.

Canticle with Gospel antiphon

The harvest is rich but the labourers are few, so ask the Lord of the harvest to send out labourers to his harvest. (Matthew 9:37)

Benedictus (p. 10)

Intercessions

As we take up again the burden of a new day,
through our sufferings may we come to see and support
the greater sufferings of others.
– Send us your Holy Spirit.

May we be united in our prayer
with all those throughout the world
who are also praying to you at this moment.
– Send us your Holy Spirit.

Deepen our spirit of prayer and praise, Lord,
and may we always give you thanks for your gifts.
– Send us your Holy Spirit.

(Personal intercessions may be added here.)

Our Father . . .

Prayer

True Light of the world, Lord Jesus Christ,
as you enlighten all men and women for their salvation,
give us grace, we pray,
to herald your coming
by preparing the ways of justice and of peace.
Who live and reign with the Father and the Holy Spirit,
God, for ever and ever. Amen.

(Morning Prayer, Tuesday, Week 2)

Let us bless the Lord.
Thanks be to God.

O God, come to our aid.
O Lord, make haste to help us.
Glory be . . .

Psalm 29 (30)

I will praise you, Lord, you have rescued me
and have not let my enemies rejoice over me.

O Lord, I cried to you for help
and you, my God, have healed me.
O Lord, you have raised my soul from the dead,
restored me to life from those who sink into the grave.

Sing psalms to the Lord, you faithful ones,
give thanks to his holy name.
God's anger lasts a moment; God's favour all through life.
At night there are tears, but joy comes with dawn.

I said to myself in my good fortune:
'Nothing will ever disturb me.'
Your favour had set me on a mountain fastness,
then you hid your face and I was put to confusion.

To you, Lord, I cried,
to my God I made appeal:
'What profit would my death be, my going down to the
   grave?
Can dust give you praise or proclaim your truth?'

The Lord listened and had pity.
The Lord came to my help.
For me you have changed my mourning into dancing,
you removed my sackcloth and clothed me with joy.
So my soul sings psalms to you unceasingly.
O Lord my God, I will thank you for ever.

Glory be . . .

Reading 2 Corinthians 12:9b-10

It is, then, about my weaknesses that I am happiest of all
to boast, so that the power of Christ may rest upon me;
and that is why I am glad of weaknesses, insults,
constraints, persecutions and distress for Christ's sake.
For it is when I am weak that I am strong.

Canticle with Gospel antiphon

The harvest is rich but the labourers are few, so ask the
Lord of the harvest to send out labourers to his harvest.
(Matthew 9:37)

Magnificat (p. 11)

Intercessions

Show your love, Lord,
to our families and our friends;
keep them in your care.
– Lord Jesus, you are our hope.

We pray for those
who are suffering in pain tonight
and for those who have today received
bad news about their health.
– Lord Jesus, you are our hope.

We thank you
for all the benefits you give us;
help us to use them wisely.
– Lord Jesus, you are our hope.

(Personal intercessions may be added here.)

Our Father . . .

Prayer

Yours is the day and yours, the night, Lord God:
let the Sun of Justice shine so steadily in our hearts,
that we may come at length
to that light where you dwell eternally.
We make this prayer through Christ our Lord. Amen.
(Evening Prayer, Tuesday, Week 2)

Let us bless the Lord.
Thanks be to God.

O Lord, open our lips,
and our mouth shall proclaim your praise.
Glory be . . .

Psalm 24 (25):1-7

To you, O Lord, I lift up my soul.
My God, I trust you, let me not be disappointed;
do not let my enemies triumph.
Those who hope in you shall not be disappointed,
but only those who wantonly break faith.

Lord, make me know your ways.
Lord, teach me your paths.
Make me walk in your truth, and teach me,
for you are God my saviour.

In you I hope all the day long
because of your goodness, O Lord.
Remember your mercy, Lord,
and the love you have shown from of old.
Do not remember the sins of my youth.
In your love remember me.

Glory be . . .

Reading 1 Corinthians 15:1-4

I want to make quite clear to you, brothers, what the
message of the Gospel that I preached to you is; you

accepted it and took your stand on it, and you are saved by it, if you keep to the message I preached to you; otherwise your coming to believe was in vain. The tradition I handed on to you in the first place, a tradition which I had myself received, was that Christ died for our sins, in accordance with the scriptures, and that he was buried; and that on the third day, he was raised to life, in accordance with the scriptures.

Canticle with Gospel antiphon

For the Son of Man himself came not to be served but to serve, and to give his life as a ransom for many. (Mark 10:45)

Benedictus (p. 10)

Intercessions

May the sacrifices we may have to make today
be made holy by the life-giving sacrifice of Christ.
– Lord Jesus, work in us today.

Help us to see the needs of our neighbours
and give us the compassion to love them.
– Lord Jesus, work in us today.

May those who design and build our cities and towns,
and those who manage our environment
always be mindful in their work
of the dignity of each human being.
– Lord Jesus, work in us today.

(Personal intercessions may be added here.)

Our Father . . .

Prayer

Shed your clear light on our hearts, Lord,
so that walking continually in the way of your
    commandments,
we may never be deceived or misled.
We make this prayer through Christ our Lord. Amen.
(Morning Prayer, Wednesday, Week 2)

Let us bless the Lord.
Thanks be to God.

O God, come to our aid.
O Lord, make haste to help us.
Glory be . . .

Psalm 138 (139):1-14

O Lord, you search me and you know me,
you know my resting and my rising,
you discern my purpose from afar.
You mark when I walk or lie down,
all my ways lie open to you.

Before ever a word is on my tongue
you know it, O Lord, through and through.
Behind and before you besiege me,
your hand ever laid upon me.
Too wonderful for me, this knowledge,
too high, beyond my reach.

O where can I go from your spirit,
or where can I flee from your face?
If I climb the heavens, you are there.
If I lie in the grave, you are there.

If I take the wings of the dawn
and dwell at the sea's furthest end,
even there your hand would lead me,
your right hand would hold me fast.

If I say: 'Let the darkness hide me
and the light around me be night,'
even darkness is not dark to you
and the night is as clear as the day.

For it was you who created my being,
knit me together in my mother's womb.
I thank you for the wonder of my being,
for the wonders of all your creation.

Glory be . . .

Reading 1 Corinthians 2:9-10

As scripture says, 'What no eye has seen and no ear has heard, what the mind of man cannot visualise; all that God has prepared for those who love him'. To us, though, God has given revelation through the Spirit, for the Spirit explores the depths of everything, even the depths of God.

Canticle with Gospel antiphon

For the Son of Man himself came not to be served but to serve, and to give his life as a ransom for many. (Mark 10:45)

Magnificat (p. 11)

Intercessions

Comfort those who today have lost a loved one.
Receive the dead into your kingdom.
– Lord, show us your mercy.

Move us to reach out in love
to those rejected by the world
and by themselves.
– Lord, show us your mercy.

We give thanks for the joy of our Christian faith;
strengthen those whose faith
causes them difficulties.
– Lord, show us your mercy.

(Personal intercessions may be added here.)

Our Father . . .

Prayer

Lord God,
whose name is holy
and whose mercy is proclaimed in every generation:
receive your people's prayer,
and let them sing your greatness with never-ending praise.
We make this prayer through Christ our Lord. Amen.

(Evening Prayer, Wednesday, Week 2)

Let us bless the Lord.
Thanks be to God.

Morning Prayer

O Lord, open our lips,
and our mouth shall proclaim your praise.
Glory be . . .

Psalm 24 (25):8-14, 22

The Lord is good and upright,
showing the path to those who stray,
guiding the humble in the right path,
and teaching the way to the poor.

God's ways are steadfastness and truth
for those faithful to the covenant decrees.
Lord, for the sake of your name
forgive my guilt, for it is great.

Those who revere the Lord
will be shown the path they should choose.
Their souls will live in happiness
and their children shall possess the land.
The Lord's friendship is for the God-fearing;
and the covenant is revealed to them.

Redeem Israel, O God, from all its distress.

Glory be . . .

Reading 1 Peter 5:5b-7

Humility towards one another must be the garment you all wear constantly, because God opposes the proud but accords his favour to the humble. Bow down, then, before the power of God now, so that he may raise you up in due time; unload all your burden on to him, since he is concerned about you.

Canticle with Gospel antiphon

Do not worry about your life and what you are to eat, nor about your body and how you are to clothe it. For life is more than food, and the body more than clothing. (Luke 12:22-23)

Benedictus (p. 10)

Intercessions

Our faith in you lightens our path for the coming day;
we pray for those who have no faith
to guide and comfort them.
– Lord, show us your love.

Lord, teach us to see you
in all our brothers and sisters.
– Lord, show us your love.

Inspire those who are creative
in art, music and word
to reflect your glory

and to bring joy and understanding into our lives.
– Lord, show us your love.

(Personal intercessions may be added here.)

Our Father . . .

Prayer

Lord God, true Light and Creator of light,
grant that faithfully pondering on all that is holy,
we may ever live in the splendour of your presence.
We make this prayer through Christ our Lord. Amen.
(Morning Prayer, Thursday, Week 2)

Let us bless the Lord.
Thanks be to God.

O God, come to our aid.
O Lord, make haste to help us.
Glory be . . .

Psalm 83 (84):2-6, 13

How lovely is your dwelling place,
Lord, God of hosts.

My soul is longing and yearning,
is yearning for the courts of the Lord.
My heart and my soul ring out their joy
to God, the living God.

The sparrow herself finds a home
and the swallow a nest for her brood;
she lays her young by your altars,
Lord of hosts, my king and my God.

They are happy, who dwell in your house,
for ever singing your praise.
They are happy, whose strength is in you,
in whose hearts are the roads to Zion.

Lord, God of hosts,
happy are those who trust in you!

Glory be . . .

Reading Romans 8:18-21

All that we suffer in the present time is nothing in comparison with the glory which is destined to be disclosed for us, for the whole creation is waiting with eagerness for the children of God to be revealed. It was not for its own purposes that creation had frustration imposed on it, but for the purposes of him who imposed it – with the intention that the whole creation itself might be freed from its slavery to corruption and brought into the same glorious freedom as the children of God.

Canticle with Gospel antiphon

Do not worry about your life and what you are to eat, nor about your body and how you are to clothe it. For life is more than food, and the body more than clothing. (Luke 12:22-23)

Magnificat (p. 11)

Intercessions

Give us the rest we need,
that we may be ever more eager to do your will.
– Lord, give us your protection.

Guide the leaders of your Church
that they may be instruments of your love and peace.
– Lord, give us your protection.

Be with those who are suffering tonight
and comfort those who are in distress.
– Lord, give us your protection.

(Personal intercessions may be added here.)

Our Father . . .

Prayer

We beseech your mercy, Lord,
as we offer you this evening praise:
keep our hearts always engaged in meditating on your law,
and grant us the light and reward of eternal life.
We make this prayer through Christ our Lord. Amen.
(Evening Prayer, Thursday, Week 2)

Let us bless the Lord.
Thanks be to God.

O Lord, open our lips,
and our mouth shall proclaim your praise.
Glory be . . .

Psalm 32 (33):1-9, 20-22

Ring out your joy to the Lord, O you just;
for praise is fitting for loyal hearts.

Give thanks to the Lord upon the harp,
with a ten-stringed lute play your songs.
Sing to the Lord a song that is new,
play loudly, with all your skill.

For the word of the Lord is faithful
and all his works done in truth.
The Lord loves justice and right
and fills the earth with love.

By God's word the heavens were made,
by the breath of his mouth all the stars.
God collects the waves of the ocean;
and stores up the depths of the sea.

Let all the earth fear the Lord,
all who live in the world stand in awe.
For God spoke; it came to be.
God commanded; it sprang into being.

Our soul is waiting for the Lord.
The Lord is our help and our shield.
Our hearts find joy in the Lord.
We trust in God's holy name.

May your love be upon us, O Lord,
as we place all our hope in you.

Glory be . . .

Reading Colossians 2:6-10

So then, as you received Jesus as Lord and Christ, now live your lives in him, be rooted in him and built up on him, held firm by the faith you have been taught, and overflowing with thanksgiving.

Make sure that no one captivates you with the empty lure of a 'philosophy' of the kind that human beings hand on, based on the principles of this world and not on Christ.

In him, in bodily form, lives divinity in all its fullness, and in him you too find your own fulfilment, in the one who is the head of every sovereignty and ruling force.

Canticle with Gospel antiphon

For this is how God loved the world: he gave his only Son, so that everyone who believes in him may not perish but may have eternal life. (John 3:16)

Benedictus (p. 10)

Intercessions

Lord of all creation,
we thank you for the gift of this new day;
fill it with your love.
– Come, Lord Jesus.

May your love guide and protect us during this day,
that we may work for your glory
and for our neighbour's good.
– Come, Lord Jesus.

Bless your Church, Lord,
as she strives to bear witness to the Good News.
– Come, Lord Jesus.

(Personal intercessions may be added here.)

Our Father . . .

Prayer

Almighty God,
as in this morning prayer we offer you our praise,
grant that, in your kingdom,
together with your saints,
we may praise you with even greater joy.
We make this prayer through Christ our Lord. Amen.
(Morning Prayer, Friday, Week 2)

Let us bless the Lord.
Thanks be to God.

O God, come to our aid.
O Lord, make haste to help us.
Glory be . . .

Psalm 114 (116)

I love the Lord, for the Lord has heard
the cry of my appeal.
The Lord was attentive to me
in the day when I called.

They surrounded me, the snares of death,
with the anguish of the tomb;
they called me, sorrow and distress.
I called on the Lord's name.

O Lord, my God, deliver me!

How gracious is the Lord, and just;
our God has compassion.
The Lord protects the simple hearts;
I was helpless so God saved me.

Turn back, my soul, to your rest
for the Lord has been good,
and has kept my soul from death,
(my eyes from tears,)
my feet from stumbling.

I will walk in the presence of the Lord
in the land of the living.

Glory be . . .

Reading James 3:17-18

. . . whereas the wisdom that comes down from above is
essentially something pure; it is also peaceable, kindly
and considerate; it is full of mercy and shows itself by
doing good; nor is there any trace of partiality or
hypocrisy in it. The peace sown by peacemakers brings a
harvest of justice.

Canticle with Gospel antiphon

For this is how God loved the world: he gave his only
Son, so that everyone who believes in him may not perish
but may have eternal life. (John 3:16)

Magnificat (p. 11)

Intercessions

Bless your Church, Lord,
that the world may see in her
the goodness of your love.
– Lord, give us your peace.

Inspire within us mutual understanding and respect;
enable us to rejoice

in the richness and diversity of human character.
– Lord, give us your peace.

Be with those who are lonely this evening
and comfort those who are afraid.
– Lord, give us your peace.

(Personal intercessions may be added here.)

Our Father . . .

Prayer

Lord God,
the Cross reveals the mystery of your love:
a stumbling block indeed for unbelief,
but the sign of your power and wisdom to us who believe.
Teach us so to contemplate your Son's glorious Passion
that we may always believe and glory in his Cross.
We make this prayer through Christ our Lord. Amen.

(Evening Prayer, Friday, Week 2)

Let us bless the Lord.
Thanks be to God.

O Lord, open our lips,
and our mouth shall proclaim your praise.
Glory be . . .

Psalm 107 (108):2-6, 13-14

My heart is ready, O God;
I will sing, sing your praise.
Awake, my soul;
awake, lyre and harp,
I will awake the dawn.

I will thank you, Lord, among the peoples,
among the nations I will praise you,
for your love reaches to the heavens
and your truth to the skies.
O God, arise above the heavens;
may your glory shine on earth!

Give us help against the foe,
for human help is vain.
With God we shall do bravely
and the Lord will trample down our foes.

Glory be . . .

Reading 1 John 3:18-24

Children, our love must be not just words or mere talk,
but something active and genuine. This will be the proof

that we belong to the truth, and it will convince us in his presence, even if our own feelings condemn us, that God is greater than our feelings and knows all things. My dear friends, if our own feelings do not condemn us, we can be fearless before God, and whatever we ask we shall receive from him, because we keep his commandments and do what is acceptable to him. His commandment is this, that we should believe in the name of his Son Jesus Christ and that we should love each other as he commanded us. Whoever keeps his commandments remains in God, and God in him. And this is the proof that he remains in us: the Spirit that he has given us.

Canticle with Gospel antiphon

Human beings live not on bread alone but on every word that comes from the mouth of God. (Matthew 4:4)

Benedictus (p. 10)

Intercessions

May your name be held holy
in all that we do today.
– Be with us, Lord, this day.

May those who work to build our society
be moved to work creatively with your Spirit.
Be with us, Lord, this day.

May those who are unable to work, or cannot find work,
be strengthened in their spirit and self-regard.
– Be with us, Lord, this day.

(Personal intercessions may be added here.)

Our Father . . .

Prayer

Let us praise you, Lord,
with voice and mind and deed:
and since life itself is your gift,
may all we have and are be yours.
We make this prayer through Christ our Lord. Amen.
(Morning Prayer, Saturday, Week 2)

Let us bless the Lord.
Thanks be to God.

O God, come to our aid.
O Lord, make haste to help us.
Glory be . . .

Psalm 39 (40):2-6

I waited, I waited for the Lord
who stooped down to me,
he heard my cry.

God drew me from the deadly pit,
from the miry clay,
and set my feet upon a rock
and made my footsteps firm.

God put a new song into my mouth,
praise of our God.
Many shall see and fear
and shall trust in the Lord.

Happy are those who have placed
their trust in the Lord
and have not gone over to the rebels
who follow false gods.

How many, O Lord my God,
are the wonders and designs
that you have worked for us;
you have no equal.

Should I proclaim and speak of them,
they are more than I can tell!

Glory be . . .

Reading Jude 20-23

But you, my dear friends, must build yourselves up on
the foundation of your most holy faith, praying in the
Holy Spirit; keep yourselves within the love of God and
wait for the mercy of our Lord Jesus Christ to give you
eternal life. To some you must be compassionate because
they are wavering; others you must save by snatching
them from the fire; to others again you must be
compassionate but wary.

Canticle with Gospel antiphon

Human beings live not on bread alone but on every word
that comes from the mouth of God. (Matthew 4:4)

Magnificat (p. 11)

Intercessions

We pray for justice in the world,
that all people may come to live in your peace.
– Lord, hear our prayer.

Have mercy on those who have lost their lives
in violence and tragedy;
take them into your peace.
– Lord, hear our prayer.

May those who provide us with entertainment and
relaxation
always be mindful of the dignity of human life.
– Lord, hear our prayer.

(Personal intercessions may be added here.)

Our Father . . .

Prayer

Send forth the light of the Holy Spirit on us,
Lord God, almighty Father,
subject as we are to your divine majesty:
so that safe from every foe,
we may always rejoice
as we celebrate your praise.
We make this prayer through Christ our Lord. Amen.
(Prayer before Noon, Saturday, Week 2)

Let us bless the Lord.
Thanks be to God.

O Lord, open our lips,
and our mouth shall proclaim your praise.
Glory be . . .

Psalm 18 (19):2-5, 8, 14-15)

The heavens proclaim the glory of God,
and the firmament shows forth the work of God's hands.
Day unto day takes up the story
and night unto night makes known the message.

No speech, no word, no voice is heard
yet their span extends through all the earth,
their words to the utmost bounds of the world.

The law of the Lord is perfect,
it revives the soul.
The rule of the Lord is to be trusted,
it gives wisdom to the simple.

From presumption restrain your servant
and let it not rule me.
Then shall I be blameless,
clean from grave sin.

May the spoken words of my mouth,
the thoughts of my heart,

win favour in your sight, O Lord,
my rescuer, my rock!

Glory be . . .

Reading Romans 12:1-2

I urge you, then, brothers, remembering the mercies of God, to offer your bodies as a living sacrifice, dedicated and acceptable to God; that is the kind of worship for you, as sensible people. Do not model your behaviour on the contemporary world, but let the renewing of your minds transform you, so that you may discern for yourselves what is the will of God – what is good and acceptable and mature.

Canticle with Gospel antiphon

The time is fulfilled, and the kingdom of God is close at hand. Repent, and believe the Gospel. (Mark 1:15)

Benedictus (p. 10)

Intercessions

As we start a new day and ask your blessing,
we pray for your special blessing
on those who are born into this world today.
– Lord Jesus, you are our strength.

May we come to see you in others,
especially in those who are rejected by society,

or by themselves.
– Lord Jesus, you are our strength.

Be with us, Lord,
as we face the demands and the temptations of this day.
– Lord Jesus, you are our strength.

(Personal intercessions may be added here.)

Our Father . . .

Prayer

King of heaven and earth, Lord God,
rule over our hearts and bodies this day.
Sanctify us,
and guide our every thought, word and deed
according to the commandments of your law,
so that now and for ever
your grace may free and save us.
We make this prayer through Christ our Lord. Amen.
(Morning Prayer, Monday, Week 3)

Let us bless the Lord.
Thanks be to God.

O God, come to our aid.
O Lord, make haste to help us.
Glory be . . .

Psalm 61 (62):6-13

In God alone be at rest, my soul;
from God comes my hope.
God alone is my rock, my stronghold,
my fortress; I stand firm.

In God is my safety and glory,
the rock of my strength.
Take refuge in God, all you people,
trusting always.
Pour out your hearts to the Lord
for God is our refuge.

Common folk are only a breath,
the great are an illusion.
Placed in the scales, they rise;
they weigh less than a breath.

Do not put your trust in oppression
nor vain hopes on plunder.
Do not set your heart on riches
even when they increase.

For God has said only one thing;
only two do I know:
that to God alone belongs power
and to you, Lord, love;
and that you repay us all
according to our deeds.

Glory be . . .

Reading 2 Corinthians 1:3-5

Blessed be the God and Father of our Lord Jesus Christ,
the merciful Father and the God who gives every possible
encouragement; he supports us in every hardship, so that
we are able to come to the support of others in every
hardship of theirs, because of the encouragement that we
ourselves receive from God. For just as the sufferings of
Christ overflow into our lives; so too does the
encouragement we receive through Christ.

Canticle with Gospel antiphon

The time is fulfilled, and the kingdom of God is close at
hand. Repent, and believe the Gospel. (Mark 1:15)

Magnificat (p. 11)

Intercessions

Guide those who serve us in leadership
in Church and state;

may they be wise in their thoughts
and just in their decisions.
– Lord, have mercy.

Bless our families, our friends and colleagues:
may your love be with them tonight.
– Christ, have mercy.

Lord, be with those who are dying;
comfort them with your love.
– Lord, have mercy.

(Personal intercessions may be added here.)

Our Father . . .

Prayer

Lord God,
it is our bounden duty to proclaim you as the Light
with whom there is no alteration or shadow of change:
enlighten our darkness as we reach the close of this day,
and in your mercy forgive us our sins.
We make this prayer through Christ our Lord. Amen.

(Evening Prayer, Monday, Week 3)

Let us bless the Lord.
Thanks be to God

Morning Prayer

O Lord, open our lips,
and our mouth shall proclaim your praise.
Glory be . . .

Psalm 45 (46)

God is for us a refuge and strength,
a helper close at hand, in time of distress,
so we shall not fear though the earth should rock,
though the mountains fall into the depths of the sea;
even though its waters rage and foam,
even though the mountains be shaken by its waves.

The Lord of hosts is with us;
the God of Jacob is our stronghold.

The waters of a river give joy to God's city,
the holy place where the Most High dwells.
God is within, it cannot be shaken;
God will help it at the dawning of the day.
Nations are in tumult, kingdoms are shaken;
God's voice roars forth, the earth shrinks away.

The Lord of hosts is with us;
the God of Jacob is our stronghold.

Come, consider the works of the Lord,
the redoubtable deeds God has done on the earth:

putting an end to wars across the earth;
breaking the bow, snapping the spear;
[burning the shields with fire.]
'Be still and know that I am God,
supreme among the nations, supreme on the earth!'

The Lord of hosts is with us;
The God of Jacob is our stronghold.

Glory be . . .

Reading Romans 8:31b-35

If God is for us, who can be against us? Since he did not
spare his own Son, but gave him up for the sake of all of
us, then can we not expect that with him he will freely
give us all his gifts? Who can bring any accusation against
those that God has chosen? When God grants saving
justice who can condemn? Are we not sure that it is Christ
Jesus, who died – yes and more, who was raised from the
dead and is at God's right hand – and who is adding his
plea for us? Can anything cut us off from the love of
Christ – can hardships or distress, or persecution, or lack of
food and clothing, or threats or violence?

Canticle with Gospel antiphon

For where two or three meet in my name, I am there
among them. (Matthew 18:20)

Benedictus (p. 10)

Intercessions

Through the Spirit, Lord,
you give us many gifts;
may we use those gifts wisely today.
– Come, Holy Spirit.

Christ came to forgive sins;
help us to forgive others as you forgive us.
– Come, Holy Spirit.

Help us to see what needs to be done
and give us the courage to do it.
– Come, Holy Spirit.

(Personal intercessions may be added here.)

Our Father . . .

Prayer

Almighty God,
to whom this world with all its goodness and beauty
    belongs,
give us grace joyfully to begin this day in your name,
and to fill it with an active love for you and our neighbour.
We make this prayer through Christ our Lord. Amen.
                    (Morning Prayer, Tuesday, Week 3)

Let us bless the Lord.
Thanks be to God.

O God, come to our aid.
O Lord, make haste to help us.
Glory be . . .

Psalm 31 (32):1-7, 11

Happy those whose offence is forgiven,
whose sin is remitted.
O happy those to whom the Lord
imputes no guilt,
in whose spirit is no guile.

I kept it secret and my frame was wasted.
I groaned all day long,
for night and day your hand
was heavy upon me.
Indeed my strength was dried up
as by the summer's heat.

But now I have acknowledged my sins;
my guilt I did not hide.
I said: 'I will confess
my offence to the Lord.'
And you, Lord, have forgiven
the guilt of my sin.

So let faithful people pray to you
in the time of need.
The floods of water may reach high

but they shall stand secure.
You are my hiding place, O Lord;
you save me from distress.
(You surround me with cries of deliverance.)

Rejoice, rejoice in the Lord,
exult, you just!
O come, ring out your joy,
all you upright of heart.

Glory be . . .

Reading Romans 15:5-7

Now the God of perseverance and encouragement give
you all the same purpose, following the example of Christ
Jesus, so that you may together give glory to the God and
Father of our Lord Jesus Christ with one heart.

Accept one another, then, for the sake of God's glory,
as Christ accepted you.

Canticle with Gospel antiphon

For where two or three meet in my name, I am there
among them. (Matthew 18:20)

Magnificat (p. 11)

Intercessions

We thank you for the gift of faith;
help those who have no faith,

or whose faith is troubled.
– Come, Lord Jesus, give us your peace.

We pray for those
who work this evening in caring for others.
– Come, Lord Jesus, come in peace.

We pray for those
who have no home to go to tonight;
ease their loneliness and give them hope.
– Come, Lord Jesus, come in peace.

(Personal intercessions may be added here.)

Our Father . . .

Prayer

Let our evening prayer rise up before your throne of
mercy, Lord,
and let your blessing come down upon us:
so that now and for ever
your grace may help and save us.
We make this prayer through Christ our Lord. Amen.

(Evening Prayer, Tuesday, Week 3)

Let us bless the Lord.
Thanks be to God.

Morning Prayer

O Lord, open our lips,
and our mouth shall proclaim your praise.
Glory be . . .

Psalm 120 (121)

I lift up my eyes to the mountains;
from where shall come my help?
My help shall come from the Lord
who made heaven and earth.

May God never allow you to stumble!
Let your guard not sleep.
Behold, neither sleeping nor slumbering,
Israel's guard.

The Lord is your guard and your shade;
and stands at your right.
By day the sun shall not smite you
nor the moon in the night.

The Lord will guard you from evil,
and will guard your soul.
The Lord will guard your going and coming
both now and for ever.

Glory be . . .

Reading Ephesians 2:4-6

But God, being rich in faithful love, through the great love with which he loved us, even when we were dead in our sins, brought us to life with Christ – it is through grace you have been saved – and raised us up with him and gave us a place with him in heaven, in Christ Jesus.

Canticle with Gospel antiphon

He said to them, 'Who do you say I am?' It was Peter who spoke up.

'The Christ of God,' he said. (Luke 9:20)

Benedictus (p. 10)

Intercessions

Lord, with the dawning of a new day
we celebrate our faith in the Resurrection;
may it give us hope.
Lord, bless your people.

Be with those who have unpleasant tasks to do today
and with those who are anxious about their work.
Lord, bless your people.

Be with those who are suffering today
in mind or body.
Lord, bless your people.

(Personal intercessions may be added here.)

Our Father . . .

Prayer

Lord God,
in your wisdom you created us,
by your providence you rule us:
penetrate our inmost being with your holy light,
so that our way of life
may always be one of faithful service to you.
We make this prayer through Christ our Lord. Amen.

(Morning Prayer, Wednesday, Week 3)

Let us bless the Lord.
Thanks be to God.

O God, come to our aid.
O Lord, make haste to help us.
Glory be . . .

Psalm 76 (77):2-14a

I cry aloud to God,
cry aloud to God to hear me.
In the day of my distress I sought the Lord.
My hands were raised at night without ceasing;
my soul refused to be consoled.
I remembered my God and I groaned.
I pondered and my spirit fainted.

You withheld sleep from my eyes.
I was troubled, I could not speak.
I thought of the days of long ago
and remembered the years long past.
At night I mused within my heart.
I pondered and my spirit questioned.

'Will the Lord reject us for ever
and no longer show favour to us?
Has God's love vanished for ever?
Has God's promise come to an end?
Does God forget to be gracious,
or in anger withhold compassion?'

I said: 'This is what causes my grief,
that the way of the Most High has changed.'
I remember the deeds of the Lord,
I remember your wonders of old,
I muse on all your works
and ponder your mighty deeds.
Your ways, O God, are holy.

Glory be . . .

Reading 1 Corinthians 13:4-7

Love is always patient and kind; love is never jealous;
love is not boastful or conceited, it is never rude and never
seeks its own advantage, it does not take offence or store up
grievances. Love does not rejoice at wrongdoing, but finds
its joy in the truth. It is always ready to make allowances,
to trust, to hope and to endure whatever comes.

Canticle with Gospel antiphon

He said to them, 'Who do you say I am?' It was Peter who
spoke up.
     'The Christ of God,' he said. (Luke 9:20)

Magnificat (p. 11)

Intercessions

Comfort those who are lonely tonight,
those who are abandoned and those in despair.
– Be with us, Lord, this night.

As we sleep this night,
others will be working for our benefit;
sustain them in their labour.
– Be with us, Lord, this night.

Strengthen our faith,
that we may be faithful
in hearing and living your Word.
– Be with us, Lord, this night.

(Personal intercessions maybe added here.)

Our Father . . .

Prayer

Let your people's cry come into your loving presence,
Lord.
Forgive them their sins,
so that by your grace they may be devoted to your
    service,
and rest secure under your protecting hand.
We make this prayer through Christ our Lord. Amen.
                        (Evening Prayer, Wednesday, Week 3)

Let us bless the Lord.
Thanks be to God.

Morning Prayer

O Lord, open our lips,
and our mouth shall proclaim your praise.
Glory be . . .

Psalm 30 (31):20-25

How great is the goodness, Lord,
that you keep for those who fear you,
that you show to those who trust you
in the sight of all.

You hide them in the shelter of your presence
from human plots;
you keep them safe within your tent
from disputing tongues.

Blessed be the Lord who has shown me
such a steadfast love
in a fortified city.

'I am far removed from your sight'
I said in my alarm.
Yet you heard the voice of my plea
when I cried for help.

Love the Lord, all you saints.
The Lord guards the faithful
but in turn will repay to the full
those who act with pride.

Be strong, let your heart take courage,
all who hope in the Lord.

Glory be . . .

Reading Ephesians 6:14-18

Stand your ground, with truth a belt round your waist,
and uprightness a breastplate, wearing for shoes on your
feet the eagerness to spread the gospel of peace and
always carrying the shield of faith so that you can use it to
quench the burning arrows of the Evil One. And then you
must take salvation as your helmet and the sword of the
Spirit, that is, the word of God. In all your prayer and
entreaty keep praying in the Spirit on every possible
occasion.

Canticle with Gospel antiphon

In all truth I tell you, whoever listens to my words,
and believes in the one who sent me, has eternal life.
(John 5:24a)

Benedictus (p. 10)

Intercessions

Lord, may we come to be more aware
of your presence among us
and to respect, in love,
the creation you have given us.
– Lord, open our hearts to your love

Christ is the Light of the world;
may that light be our guide
through the dark moments of the day.
– Lord, open our hearts to your love.

Lord, may we be generous of heart
to those we meet today.
– Lord, open our hearts to your love.

(Personal intercessions may be added here.)

Our Father . . .

Prayer

Almighty, ever-living God,
shed the light of your glory
on the peoples who are living in the shadow of death,
as you did long ago,
when our Lord Jesus Christ, the Sun of Justice,
came among us from on high.
We make this prayer through Christ our Lord. Amen.
(Morning Prayer, Thursday, Week 3)

Let us bless the Lord.
Thanks be to God.

O God, come to our aid.
O Lord, make haste to help us.
Glory be . . .

Psalm 55 (56):2-7, 10b-14

Have mercy on me God, foes crush me;
they fight me all day long and oppress me.
My foes crush me all day long,
for many fight proudly against me.

When I fear, I will trust in you,
in God whose word I praise.
In God I trust, I shall not fear;
what can mere mortals do to me?

All day long they distort my words,
all their thought is to harm me.
They band together in ambush,
track me down and seek my life.

This I know, that God is on my side.
In God, whose word I praise,
(in the Lord, whose word I praise,)
in God I trust; I shall not fear;
what can mere mortals do to me?

I am bound by the vows I have made you.
O God, I will offer you praise

for you rescued my soul from death,
you kept my feet from stumbling
that I may walk in the presence of God
and enjoy the light of the living.

Glory be . . .

Reading 1 John 1:1-4

Something which has existed since the beginning, which we have heard, which we have seen with our own eyes, which we have watched and touched with our own hands, the Word of life – this is our theme.

That life was made visible; we saw it and are giving our testimony, declaring to you the eternal life, which was present to the Father and has been revealed to us. We are declaring to you what we have seen and heard, so that you too may share our life. Our life is shared with the Father and his Son Jesus Christ. We are writing this to you so that our joy may be complete.

Canticle with Gospel antiphon

In all truth I tell you, whoever listens to my words, and believes in the one who sent me, has eternal life. (John 5:24a)

Magnificat (p. 11)

Intercessions

Keep your Church faithful
in proclaiming your message

of forgiveness, hope and love.
– Lord Jesus, you are our peace.

Comfort and strengthen those
who have received sad or troubling news today.
– Lord Jesus, you are our peace.

Be with all those throughout the world
who are united this evening
in praying in Christ's name.
– Lord Jesus, you are our peace.

(Personal intercessions may be added here.)

Our Father . . .

Prayer

We offer you, Lord, our thanksgiving
at the close of this day:
in your mercy forgive the faults we have committed
through human frailty.
We make this prayer through Christ our Lord. Amen.
(Evening Prayer, Thursday, Week 3)

Let us bless the Lord.
Thanks be to God.

O Lord, open our lips,
and our mouth shall proclaim your praise.
Glory be . . .

Psalm 17 (18):2-4, 29-33

I love you, Lord, my strength,
my rock, my fortress, my saviour.
God, you are the rock where I take refuge;
my shield, my mighty help, my stronghold.
Lord, you are worthy of all praise,
when I call I am saved from my foes.

You, O Lord, are my lamp,
my God who lightens my darkness.
With you I can break through any barrier,
with my God I can scale any wall.

Your ways, O God, are perfect;
your word, O Lord, is purest gold.
You indeed are the shield
of all who make you their refuge.

For who is God but you, Lord?
Who is a rock but you, my God?
You who gird me with strength
and make the path safe before me.

Glory be . . .

Reading Colossians 3:1-4

Since you have been raised up to be with Christ, you must look for the things that are above, where Christ is, sitting at God's right hand. Let your thoughts be on things above, not on the things that are on the earth, because you have died, and now the life you have is hidden with Christ in God. But when Christ is revealed – and he is your life – you, too, will be revealed with him in glory.

Canticle with Gospel antiphon

Blessed are the peacemakers: they shall be recognised as children of God. (Matthew 5:9)

Benedictus (p. 10)

Intercessions

You have renewed us in baptism;
renew us again today in your love.
– Lord, we trust in you.

Strengthen those, Lord,
who are in need of our prayers this morning,
especially those unable to care for themselves.
– Lord, we trust in you.

May we bring joy and hope,
not sorrow or pain,

to those we meet today.
– Lord, we trust in you.

(Personal intercessions may be added here.)

Our Father . . .

Prayer

Almighty Father,
let your light so penetrate our minds,
that walking by your commandments
we may always follow you, our leader and guide.
We make this prayer through Christ our Lord. Amen.
(Morning Prayer, Friday, Week 3)

Let us bless the Lord.
Thanks be to God.

O God, come to our aid.
O Lord, make haste to help us.
Glory be . . .

Psalm 146 (147)

Sing praise to the Lord who is good;
sing to our God who is loving:
to God our praise is due.

The Lord builds up Jerusalem
and brings back Israel's exiles,
God heals the broken-hearted,
and binds up all their wounds.
God fixes the number of the stars
and calls each one by its name.

Our Lord is great and almighty;
God's wisdom can never be measured.
The Lord raises the lowly;
and humbles the wicked to the dust.
O sing to the Lord, giving thanks;
sing psalms to our God with the harp.

God covers the heavens with clouds,
and prepares the rain for the earth;
making mountains sprout with grass
and with plants to serve our needs.
God provides the beasts with their food
and the young ravens when they cry.

God takes no delight in horses' power
nor pleasure in warriors' strength.
The Lord delights in those who revere him,
in those who wait for his love.

Glory be . . .

Reading Romans 11:33-36

How rich and deep are the wisdom and knowledge of
God! We cannot reach to the root of his decisions or his
ways. Who has ever known the mind of the Lord? Who
has ever been his adviser? Who has given anything to
him, so that his presents come only as a debt returned?
Everything there is comes from him and is caused by him
and exists for him. To him be glory for ever! Amen.

Canticle with Gospel antiphon

Blessed are the peacemakers: they shall be recognised as
children of God. (Matthew 5:9)

Magnificat (p. 11)

Intercessions

We pray for Christian families;
may they be strengthened in their witness of faith.
– Bless your people, Lord.

We give thanks for the nourishment you give us
and pray for the relief of hunger and poverty.
– Bless your people, Lord.

Give rest to those who have died today;
welcome them into your peace.
– Bless your people, Lord.

(Personal intercessions may be added here.)

Our Father . . .

Prayer

Holy Father and Lord,
you willed that Christ your Son,
should be the price of our salvation.
Give us grace so to live,
that through sharing his sufferings
we may be strengthened by the power of his resurrection,
who lives and reigns with you and the Holy Spirit,
God, for ever and ever. Amen.

(Evening Prayer, Friday, Week 3)

Let us bless the Lord.
Thanks be to God.

O Lord, open our lips,
and our mouth shall proclaim your praise.
Glory be . . .

Psalm 97 (98)

Sing a new song to the Lord
who has worked wonders;
whose right hand and holy arm
have brought salvation.

The Lord has made known salvation;
has shown justice to the nations;
has remembered truth and love
for the house of Israel.

All the ends of the earth have seen
the salvation of our God.
Shout to the Lord, all the earth,
ring out your joy.

Sing psalms to the Lord with the harp
with the sound of music.
With trumpets and the sound of the horn
acclaim the King, the Lord.

Let the sea and all within it, thunder;
the world, and all its peoples.
Let the rivers clap their hands
and the hills ring out their joy

at the presence of the Lord, who comes,
who comes to rule the earth.
God will rule the world with justice
and the peoples with fairness.

Glory be . . .

Reading Romans 12:14-18

Bless your persecutors; never curse them, bless them. Rejoice with others when they rejoice, and be sad with those in sorrow. Give the same consideration to all others alike. Pay no regard to social standing, but meet humble people on their own terms. Do not congratulate yourself on your own wisdom. Never pay back evil with evil, but bear in mind the ideals that all regard with respect. As much as is possible, and to the utmost of your ability, be at peace with everyone.

Canticle with Gospel antiphon

The Sabbath was made for man, not man for the Sabbath; so the Son of Man is master even of the Sabbath. (Mark 2:27)

Benedictus (p. 10)

Intercessions

As we take up again the burden of a new day,
through our sufferings may we come to see and support

the greater sufferings of others.
– Send us your Holy Spirit.

May we be united in our prayer
with all those throughout the world
who are also praying to you at this moment.
– Send us your Holy Spirit.

Deepen our spirit of prayer and praise, Lord,
and may we always give you thanks for your gifts.
Send us your Holy Spirit.

(Personal intercessions may be added here.)

Our Father . . .

Prayer

Lord God,
source and origin of our salvation,
make our lives here on earth so proclaim your glory,
that we may praise you without ceasing in heaven.
We make this prayer through Christ our Lord. Amen.

(Morning Prayer, Saturday, Week 3)

Let us bless the Lord.
Thanks be to God.

O God, come to our aid.
O Lord, make haste to help us.
Glory be . . .

Psalm 24 (25)1-2a, 15-22)

To you, O Lord, I lift up my soul.
My God, I trust you, let me not be disappointed;

My eyes are always on the Lord,
who will rescue my feet from the snare.
Turn to me and have mercy
for I am lonely and poor.

Relieve the anguish of my heart
and set me free from my distress.
See my affliction and my toil
and take all my sins away.

See how many are my foes,
how violent their hatred for me.
Preserve my life and rescue me.
Do not disappoint me, you are my refuge.
May innocence and uprightness protect me,
for my hope is in you, O Lord.

Redeem Israel, O God, from all its distress.

Glory be . . .

Reading 1 Corinthians 4:1-5

People should think of us as Christ's servants, stewards entrusted with the mysteries of God. In such a matter, what is expected of stewards is that each one should be found trustworthy. It is of no importance to me how you or any other human court may judge me: I will not even be the judge of my own self. It is true that my conscience does not reproach me, but that is not enough to justify me: it is the Lord who is my judge. For that reason, do not judge anything before the due time, until the Lord comes; he will bring to light everything that is hidden in darkness and reveal the designs of all hearts. Then everyone will receive from God the appropriate commendation.

Canticle with Gospel antiphon

The Sabbath was made for man, not man for the Sabbath; so the Son of Man is master even of the Sabbath. (Mark 2:27)

Magnificat (p. 11)

Intercessions

Show your love, Lord,
to our families and our friends;
keep them in your care.
– Lord Jesus, you are our hope.

We pray for those who are suffering
in pain tonight

and for those who have today received
bad news about their health.
– Lord Jesus, you are our hope.

We thank you for all the benefits you give us;
help us to use them wisely.
– Lord Jesus, you are our hope.

(Personal intercessions may be added here.)

Our Father . . .

Prayer

Lord, in answer to our prayer
give us patience in suffering hardships
after the example of your Only-begotten Son,
who lives and reigns for ever and ever. Amen.

(Afternoon Prayer, Thursday, Week 4)

Let us bless the Lord.
Thanks be to God.

O Lord, open our lips,
and our mouth shall proclaim your praise.
Glory be . . .

Psalm 91 (92)

It is good to give thanks to the Lord,
to make music to your name, O Most High,
to proclaim your love in the morning
and your truth in the watches of the night,
on the ten-stringed lyre and the lute,
with the murmuring sound of the harp.

Your deeds, O Lord, have made me glad;
for the work of your hands I shout with joy.
O Lord, how great are your works!
How deep are your designs!
The stupid cannot know this
and the foolish cannot understand.

Though the wicked spring up like grass
and all who do evil thrive,
they are doomed to be eternally destroyed.
But you, Lord, are eternally on high.
See how your enemies perish;
all doers of evil are scattered.

To me you give the wild ox's strength;
you anoint me with the purest oil.
My eyes looked in triumph on my foes;
my ears heard gladly of their fall.

The just will flourish like the palm tree
and grow like a Lebanon cedar.

Planted in the house of the Lord
they will flourish in the courts of our God,
still bearing fruit when they are old,
still full of sap, still green,
to proclaim that the Lord is just.
My rock, in whom there is no wrong.

Glory be . . .

Reading Romans 12:8b-13

When you give, you should give generously from the
heart; if you are put in charge, you must be conscientious;
if you do works of mercy, let it be because you enjoy
doing them. Let love be without any pretence. Avoid
what is evil; stick to what is good. In brotherly love let
your feelings of deep affection for one another come to
expression and regard others as more important than
yourself. In the service of the Lord, work not half-
heartedly but with conscientiousness and an eager spirit.
Be joyful in hope, persevere in hardship; keep praying
regularly; share with any of God's holy people who are in
need; look for opportunities to be hospitable.

Canticle with Gospel antiphon

Whoever welcomes the one I send, welcomes me, and
whoever welcomes me, welcomes the one who sent me.
(John 13:20)

Benedictus (p 10)

Intercessions

May the sacrifices we may have to make today
be made holy by the life-giving sacrifice of Christ.
– Lord Jesus, work in us today.

Help us to see the needs of our neighbours
and give us the compassion to love them.
– Lord Jesus, work in us today.

May those who design and build our cities and towns,
and those who manage our environment
always be mindful in their work
of the dignity of each human being.
– Lord Jesus, work in us today.

(Personal intercessions may be added here.)

Our Father . . .

Prayer

Lord God,
who entrusted the earth to us
to till it and care for it,
and made the sun to serve our needs:
give us grace this day to work faithfully for your glory
and for our neighbours' good.
We make this prayer through Christ our Lord. Amen.

(Morning Prayer, Monday, Week 4)

Let us bless the Lord.
Thanks be to God.

O God, come to our aid.
O Lord, make haste to help us.
Glory be . . .

Psalm 50 (51):3-6a, 12-17)

Have mercy on me, God, in your kindness.
In your compassion blot out my offence.
O wash me more and more from my guilt
and cleanse me from my sin.

My offences truly I know them;
my sin is always before me.
Against you, you alone, have I sinned;
what is evil in your sight I have done.

A pure heart create for me, O God,
put a steadfast spirit within me,
Do not cast me away from your presence,
nor deprive me of your Holy Spirit.

Give me again the joy of your help;
with a spirit of fervour sustain me,
that I may teach transgressors your ways
and sinners may return to you.

O rescue me, God, my helper,
and my tongue shall ring out your goodness.

O Lord, open my lips
and my mouth shall declare your praise.

Glory be . . .

Reading Hebrews 12:1b-2

Throw off everything that weighs us down and the sin
that clings so closely, and with perseverance keep running
in the race which lies ahead of us. Let us keep our eyes
fixed on Jesus, who leads us in our faith and brings it to
perfection: for the sake of the joy which lay ahead of him,
he endured the cross, disregarding the shame of it, and
has taken his seat at the right of God's throne.

Canticle with Gospel antiphon

Whoever welcomes the one I send, welcomes me, and
whoever welcomes me, welcomes the one who sent me.
(John 13:20)

Magnificat (p. 11)

Intercessions

Comfort those who today have lost a loved one.
Receive the dead into your kingdom.
– Lord, show us your mercy.

Move us to reach out in love
to those rejected by the world and by themselves.
– Lord, show us your mercy.

We give thanks for the joy of our Christian faith;
strengthen those whose faith causes them difficulties.
– Lord, show us your mercy.

(Personal intercessions may be added here.)

Our Father . . .

Prayer

Stay with us, Lord Jesus, as evening falls:
be our companion on our way.
In your mercy inflame our hearts and raise our hope,
so that, in union with our brethren,
we may recognise you in the scriptures,
and in the breaking of bread.
Who live and reign with the Father and the Holy Spirit,
God, for ever and ever. Amen.

(Evening Prayer, Monday, Week 4)

Let us bless the Lord.
Thanks be to God.

Morning Prayer

O Lord, open our lips,
and our mouth shall proclaim your praise.
Glory be . . .

Psalm 121 (122)

I rejoiced when I heard them say:
'Let us go to God's house.'
And now our feet are standing
within your gates, O Jerusalem.

Jerusalem is built as a city
strongly compact.
It is there that the tribes go up,
the tribes of the Lord.

For Israel's law it is,
there to praise the Lord's name.
There were set the thrones of judgement
of the house of David.

For the peace of Jerusalem pray:
'Peace be to your homes!
May peace reign in your walls,
in your palaces, peace!'

For the love of my family and friends
I say: 'Peace upon you.'

For love of the house of the Lord
I will ask for your good.

Glory be . . .

Reading 2 Timothy 1:6-9

I am reminding you now to fan into a flame the gift of God that you possess through the laying on of my hands. God did not give us a spirit of timidity, but the Spirit of power and love and self-control. So you are never to be ashamed of witnessing to our Lord, or ashamed of me for being his prisoner; but share in my hardships for the sake of the Gospel, relying on the power of God who has saved us and called us holy – not because of anything we ourselves had done but for his own purpose and by his own grace.

Canticle with Gospel antiphon

You must therefore set no bounds to your love, just as your heavenly Father sets none to his. (Matthew 5:48b)

Benedictus (p. 10)

Intercessions

Our faith in you lightens our path
for the coming day;
we pray for those who have no faith
to guide and comfort them.
– Lord, show us your love.

Lord, teach us to see you
in all our brothers and sisters.
– Lord, show us your love.

Inspire those who are creative in art, music and word
to reflect your glory
and to bring joy and understanding into our lives.
– Lord, show us your love.

(Personal intercessions may be added here.)

Our Father . . .

Prayer

Increase in us, Lord, your gift of faith,
so that the praise we offer you
may ever yield its fruit from heaven.
We make this prayer through Christ our Lord. Amen.
(Morning Prayer, Tuesday, Week 4)

Let us bless the Lord.
Thanks be to God.

O God, come to our aid.
O Lord, make haste to help us.
Glory be . . .

Psalm 103 (104):1-2, 24-31a

Bless the Lord, my soul!
Lord God, how great you are,
clothed in majesty and glory,
wrapped in light as in a robe!

How many are your works, O Lord!
In wisdom you have made them all.
The earth is full of your riches.

There is the sea, vast and wide,
with its moving swarms past counting,
living things great and small.
The ships are moving there
and the monsters you made to play with.

All of those look to you
to give them their food in due season.
You give it, they gather it up;
you open your hand, they have their fill.

You hide your face, they are dismayed;
you take back your spirit, they die,

returning to the dust from which they came.
You send forth your spirit, they are created;
and you renew the face of the earth.

May the glory of the Lord last for ever!

Glory be . . .

Reading Ephesians 4:3-6

Take every care to preserve the unity of the Spirit by the peace that binds you together. There is one body, one Spirit, just as one hope is the goal of your calling by God. There is one Lord, one faith, one baptism, and one God and Father of all, over all, through all and within all.

Canticle with Gospel antiphon

You must therefore set no bounds to your love, just as your heavenly Father sets none to his. (Matthew 5:48b)

Magnificat (p.

Intercessions

Give us the rest we need,
that we may be ever more eager to do your will.
– Lord, give us your protection.

Guide the leaders of your Church
that they may be instruments of your love and peace.
– Lord, give us your protection.

131

Be with those who are suffering tonight
and comfort those who are in distress.
– Lord, give us your protection.

(Personal intercessions may be added here.)

Our Father . . .

Prayer

As we pray before you, Lord,
we ask you, in your mercy, for the grace
always to ponder in our hearts
what we proclaim with our lips.
We make this prayer through Christ our Lord. Amen.
(Evening Prayer, Tuesday, Week 4)

Let us bless the Lord.
Thanks be to God.

Morning Prayer

O Lord, open our lips,
and our mouth shall proclaim your praise.
Glory be . . .

Psalm 95 (96)

O sing a new song to the Lord,
sing to the Lord all the earth.
O sing to the Lord, bless his name.

Proclaim God's help day by day,
tell among the nations his glory
and his wonders among all the peoples.

The Lord is great and worthy of praise,
to be feared above all gods;
the gods of the heathens are naught.

It was the Lord who made the heavens.
His are majesty and honour and power
and splendour in the holy place.

Give the Lord, you families of peoples,
give the Lord glory and power;
give the Lord the glory of his name.

Bring an offering and enter God's courts,
worship the Lord in the temple.
O earth, stand in fear of the Lord.

Proclaim to the nations: 'God is king.'
The world was made firm in its place;
God will judge the people in fairness.

Let the heavens rejoice and earth be glad,
let the sea and all within it thunder praise,
let the land and all it bears rejoice,
all the trees of the wood shout for joy

at the presence of the Lord who comes,
who comes to rule the earth
comes with justice to rule the world,
and to judge the peoples with truth.

Glory be . . .

Reading Ephesians 1:17-18

May the God of our Lord Jesus Christ, the Father of glory,
give you a spirit of wisdom and perception of what is
revealed, to bring you to full knowledge of him. May he
enlighten the eyes of your mind so that you can see what
hope his call holds for you, how rich is the glory of the
heritage he offers among his holy people.

Canticle with Gospel antiphon

If anyone wants to be first, he must make himself last of
all and servant of all. (Mark 9:35b)

Benedictus (p. 10)

Intercessions

Lord of all creation,
we thank you for the gift of this new day;
fill it with your love.
– Come, Lord Jesus.

May your love guide and protect us during this day,
that we may work for your glory
and for our neighbour's good.
– Come, Lord Jesus.

Bless your Church, Lord,
as she strives to bear witness to the Good News.
– Come, Lord Jesus.

(Personal intercessions may be added here.)

Our Father . . .

Prayer

Remember, Lord, your solemn covenant,
renewed and consecrated by the blood of the Lamb,
so that your people may obtain forgiveness for their sins,
and a continued growth in grace.
We make our prayer through Christ our Lord. Amen.
(Morning Prayer, Wednesday, Week 4)

Let us bless the Lord.
Thanks be to God.

O God, come to our aid.
O Lord, make haste to help us.
Glory be . . .

Psalm 27 (28):1-2, 6-9)

To you, O Lord, I call,
my rock, hear me.
If you do not heed I shall become
like those in the grave.

Hear the voice of my pleading
as I call for help,
as I lift up my hands in prayer
to your holy place.

Praise to you, Lord, you have heard
my cry, my appeal.
You, Lord, are my strength and my shield;
in you my heart trusts.
I was helped, my heart rejoices
and I praise you with my song.

Lord, you are the strength of your people,
a fortress where your anointed finds refuge.
Save your people; bless Israel your heritage.
Be their shepherd and carry them for ever.

Glory be . . .

Reading 1 Timothy 6:17-19

Instruct those who are rich in this world's goods that they should not be proud and should set their hopes not on money, which is untrustworthy, but on God who gives us richly all that we need for our happiness. They are to do good and be rich in good works, generous in giving and always ready to share – this is the way they can amass a good capital sum for the future if they want to possess the only life that is real.

Canticle with Gospel antiphon

If anyone wants to be first, he must make himself last of all and servant of all. (Mark 9:35b)

Magnificat (p. 11)

Intercessions

Bless your Church, Lord,
that the world may see in her
the goodness of your love.
– Lord, give us your peace.

Inspire within us mutual understanding and respect;
enable us to rejoice
in the richness and diversity of human character.
– Lord, give us your peace.

Be with those who are lonely this evening
and comfort those who are afraid.
– Lord, give us your peace.

(Personal intercessions may be added here.)

Our Father . . .

Prayer

Remember your people, Lord, and show them mercy:
as you satisfy the hungry with food from heaven,
enrich our poverty from your abundance.
We make this prayer through Christ our Lord. Amen.
(Evening Prayer, Wednesday, Week 4)

Let us bless the Lord.
Thanks be to God.

O Lord, open our lips,
and our mouth shall proclaim your praise.
Glory be . . .

Psalm 36 (37):1-9

Do not fret because of the wicked;
do not envy those who do evil,
for they wither quickly like grass
and fade like the green of the fields.

If you trust in the Lord and do good,
then you will live in the land and be secure.
If you find your delight in the Lord,
he will grant your heart's desire.

Commit your life to the Lord,
be confident, and God will act,
so that your justice breaks forth like the light,
your cause like the noonday sun.

Be still before the Lord and wait in patience;
do not fret at those who prosper;
those who make evil plots
to bring down the needy and the poor.

Calm your anger and forget your rage;
do not fret, it only leads to evil.
For those who do evil shall perish;
those waiting for the Lord shall inherit the land.

Glory be . . .

Reading James 1:22-25

But you must do what the Word tells you and not just listen to it and deceive yourselves. Anyone who listens to the Word and takes no action is like someone who looks at his own features in a mirror and, once he has seen what he looks like, goes off and immediately forgets it. But anyone who looks steadily at the perfect law of freedom and keeps to it – not listening and forgetting, but putting it into practice – will be blessed in every undertaking.

Canticle with Gospel antiphon

I am the Way; I am Truth and Life. No one can come to the Father except through me. (John 14:6)

Benedictus (p. 10)

Intercessions

May your name be held holy
in all that we do today.
– Be with us, Lord, this day.

May those who work to build our society
be moved to work creatively with your Spirit.
– Be with us, Lord, this day.

May those who are unable to work,
or cannot find work,
be strengthened in their spirit and self-regard.
– Be with us, Lord, this day.

(Personal intercessions may be added here.)

Our Father . . .

Prayer

Grant us, Lord, a true knowledge of salvation,
so that, freed from fear and from the power of our foes,
we may serve you faithfully,
all the days of our life.
We make this prayer through Christ our Lord. Amen.
(Morning Prayer, Thursday, Week 4)

Let us bless the Lord.
Thanks be to God.

Evening Prayer

O God, come to our aid.
O Lord, make haste to help us.
Glory be . . .

Psalm 112 (113)

Praise, O servants of the Lord,
praise the name of the Lord!
May the name of the Lord be blessed
both now and for evermore!
From the rising of the sun to its setting
praised be the name of the Lord!

High above all nations is the Lord,
above the heavens God's glory.
Who is like the Lord, our God,
the one enthroned on high,
who stoops from the heights to look down,
to look down upon heaven and earth?

From the dust God lifts up the lowly,
from the dungheap God raises the poor
to set them in the company of rulers,
yes, with the rulers of the people.
To the childless wife God gives a home
and gladdens her heart with children.

Glory be . . .

Reading Romans 8:26-27

The Spirit, too, comes to help us in our weakness, for, when we do not know how to pray properly, then the Spirit personally makes our petitions for us in groans that cannot be put into words; and he who can see into all hearts knows what the Spirit means because the prayers that the Spirit makes for God's holy people are always in accordance with the mind of God.

Canticle with Gospel antiphon

I am the Way; I am Truth and Life. No one can come to the Father except through me. (John 14:6)

Magnificat (p. 11)

Intercessions

We pray for justice in the world,
that all people may come to live in your peace.
– Lord, hear our prayer.

Have mercy on those who have lost their lives
in violence and tragedy;
take them into your peace.
– Lord, hear our prayer.

May those who provide us
with entertainment and relaxation
always be mindful of the dignity of human life.
– Lord, hear our prayer.

(Personal intercessions may be added here.)

Our Father . . .

Prayer

Listen favourably to our evening prayer, Lord,
and grant that as we follow your Son's example,
we may, by perseverance, yield a harvest of good works.
We make this prayer through Christ our Lord. Amen.

(Evening Prayer, Thursday, Week 4)

Let us bless the Lord.
Thanks be to God.

Morning Prayer

O Lord, open our lips,
and our mouth shall proclaim your praise.
Glory be . . .

Psalm 23 (24):1-6

The Lord's is the earth and its fullness
the world and all its peoples.
It is God who set it on the seas;
who made it firm on the waters.

Who shall climb the mountain of the Lord?
Who shall stand in God's holy place?
Those with clean hands and pure heart,
who desire not worthless things,
(who have not sworn so as to deceive their neighbour).

They shall receive blessings from the Lord
and reward from the God who saves them.
These are the ones who seek,
seek the face of the God of Jacob.

Glory be . . .

Reading 1 Peter 4:10-11

Each one of you has received a special grace, so, like good
stewards responsible for all these varied graces of God,

put it at the service of others. If anyone is a speaker, let it be as the words of God, if anyone serves, let it be as in strength granted by God; so that in everything God may receive the glory, through Jesus Christ, since to him alone belong all glory and power for ever and ever. Amen.

Canticle with Gospel antiphon

So always treat others as you would like them to treat you; that is the Law and the Prophets. (Matthew 7:12)

Benedictus (p. 10)

Intercessions

As we start a new day and ask your blessing,
we pray for your special blessing
on those who are born into this world today.
– Lord Jesus, you are our strength.

May we come to see you in others,
especially in those who are rejected by society,
or by themselves.
– Lord Jesus, you are our strength.

Be with us, Lord,
as we face the demands and the temptations of this day.
– Lord Jesus, you are our strength.

(Personal intercessions may be added here.)

Our Father . . .

Prayer

Lord God,
bestow a full measure of your grace on us
who are gathered here in prayer.
As you work within us
to keep us in the path of your commandments,
may we receive consolation in this present life
and eternal joys in the next.
We make this prayer through Christ our Lord. Amen.

(Morning Prayer, Friday, Week 4)

Let us bless the Lord.
Thanks be to God.

O God, come to our aid.
O Lord, make haste to help us.
Glory be . . .

Psalm 41 (42):2-6

Like the deer that yearns
for running streams,
so my soul is yearning
for you, my God.

My soul is thirsting for God,
the God of my life;
when can I enter and see
the face of my God?

My tears have become my bread,
by night, by day,
as I hear it said all the day long:
'Where is your God?'

These things will I remember
as I pour out my soul:
how I would lead the rejoicing crowd
into the house of God,
amid cries of gladness and thanksgiving,
the throng wild with joy.

Why are you cast down, my soul,
why groan within me?
Hope in God; I will praise yet again,
my saviour and my God.

Glory be . . .

Reading 2 Corinthians 13:5-9

Put yourselves to the test to make sure you are in the
faith. Examine yourselves. Do you not recognise
yourselves as people in whom Jesus Christ is present? –
unless, that is, you fail the test. But we, as I hope you will
come to recognise, do not fail the test. It is our prayer to
God that you may do nothing wrong – not so that we
have the credit of passing a test, but because you will be
doing what is right, even if we do not pass the test. We
have no power to resist the truth; only to further the
truth; and we are delighted to be weak if only you are
strong. What we ask in our prayers is that you should be
made perfect.

Canticle with Gospel antiphon

So always treat others as you would like them to treat
you; that is the Law and the Prophets. (Matthew 7:12)

Magnificat (p. 11)

Intercessions

Guide those who serve us in leadership
in Church and state;

may they be wise in their thoughts
and just in their decisions.
– Lord, have mercy.

Bless our families, our friends and colleagues:
may your love be with them tonight.
– Christ, have mercy.

Lord, be with those who are dying;
comfort them with your love.
– Lord, have mercy.

(Personal intercessions may be added here.)

Our Father . . .

Prayer

God of power and mercy,
who willed that Christ your Son should suffer for the
salvation of all the world,
grant that your people may strive to offer themselves to
you as a living sacrifice,
and may be filled with the fullness of your love.
We make this prayer through Christ our Lord. Amen.

(Evening Prayer, Friday, Week 4)

Let us bless the Lord.
Thanks be to God.

O Lord, open our lips,
and our mouth shall proclaim your praise.
Glory be . . .

Psalm 88 (89):2-9, 53

I will sing for ever of your love, O Lord;
through all ages my mouth will proclaim your truth.
Of this I am sure, that your love lasts for ever,
that your truth is firmly established as the heavens.

'With my chosen one I have made a covenant;
I have sworn to David my servant:
I will establish your dynasty for ever
and set up your throne through all ages.'

The heavens proclaim your wonders, O Lord;
the assembly of your holy ones proclaims your truth.
For who in the skies can compare with the Lord;
who is like the Lord among the children of God?

A God to be feared in the council of the holy ones,
great and dreadful, revered above all.
O Lord God of hosts, who is your equal?
You are mighty, O Lord, and truth is your garment.

Blessed be the Lord for ever. Amen. Amen!

Glory be . . .

Reading Colossians 3:12-15

As the chosen of God, then, the holy people whom he loves, you are to be clothed in heartfelt compassion, in generosity and humility, gentleness and patience. Bear with one another; forgive each other if one of you has a complaint against another. The Lord has forgiven you; you must now do the same. Over all these clothes, put on love, the perfect bond. And may the peace of Christ reign in your hearts, because it is for this that you were called together in one body. Always be thankful.

Canticle with Gospel antiphon

For wherever your treasure is, that is where your heart will be too. (Luke 12:34)

Benedictus (p. 10)

Intercessions

Through the Spirit, Lord,
you give us many gifts;
may we use those gifts wisely today.
– Come, Holy Spirit.

Christ came to forgive sins;
help us to forgive others
as you forgive us.
– Come, Holy Spirit.

Help us to see what needs to be done
and give us the courage to do it.
– Come, Holy Spirit.

(Personal intercessions may be added here.)

Our Father . . .

Prayer

All-powerful, eternal God,
splendour of true light and never-ending day:
at this return of the morning hour
chase away the night of sin,
and fill our minds with the glory of your coming.
We make this prayer through Christ our Lord. Amen.
(Morning Prayer, Saturday, Week 4)

Let us bless the Lord.
Thanks be to God.

DAY 24 *Evening Prayer*

O God, come to our aid.
O Lord, make haste to help us.
Glory be . . .

Psalm 102 (103):1-10, 21-22)

My soul, give thanks to the Lord,
all my being, bless God's holy name.
My soul, give thanks to the Lord
and never forget all God's blessings.

It is God who forgives all your guilt,
who heals every one of your ills,
who redeems your life from the grave,
who crowns you with love and compassion,
who fills your life with good things,
renewing your youth like an eagle's.

The Lord does deeds of justice,
gives judgement for all who are oppressed.
The Lord's ways were made known to Moses;
the Lord's deeds to Israel's children.

The Lord is compassion and love,
slow to anger and rich in mercy.
The Lord will not always chide,
will not be angry forever.
God does not treat us according to our sins
nor repay us according to our faults.

Give thanks to the Lord, all you hosts,
you servants who do God's will.
Give thanks to the Lord, all his works,
in every place where God rules.
My soul, give thanks to the Lord!

Glory be . . .

Reading 1 Peter 1:3-5

Blessed be God the Father of our Lord Jesus Christ, who
in his great mercy has given us a new birth into a living
hope through the resurrection of Jesus Christ from the
dead and into a heritage that can never be spoilt or soiled
and never fade away. It is reserved in heaven for you who
are being kept safe by God's power through faith until the
salvation which has been prepared is revealed at the final
point of time.

Canticle with Gospel antiphon

For wherever your treasure is, that is where your heart
will be too. (Luke 12:34)

Magnificat (p. 11)

Intercessions

We thank you for the gift of faith;
help those who have no faith, or whose faith is troubled.
– Come, Lord Jesus, give us your peace.

We pray for those who work this evening
in caring for others.
– Come, Lord Jesus, come in peace.

We pray for those who have no home to go to tonight;
ease their loneliness and give them hope.
– Come, Lord Jesus, come in peace.

(Personal intercessions may be added here.)

Our Father . . .

Prayer

Lord God,
living light of eternal love,
grant that always aglow with charity,
we may love you above all else
and our sisters and brothers for your sake,
with one and the self-same love.
We make this prayer through Christ our Lord. Amen.
(Midday Prayer, Saturday, Week 4)

Let us bless the Lord.
Thanks be to God.

O Lord, open our lips,
and our mouth shall proclaim your praise.
Glory be. . .

Psalm 65 (66) 1-9

Cry out with joy to God all the earth,
O sing to the glory of his name
rendering glorious praise.
Say to God: 'How tremendous your deeds!

Because of the greatness of your strength
your enemies cringe before you.
Before you all the earth shall bow,
shall sing to you, sing to your name!'

Come and see the works of God,
tremendous deeds for the people.
God turned the sea into dry land,
they passed through the river dry-shod.

Let our joy then be in the Lord,
who rules forever in power,
whose eyes keep watch over nations;
let rebels not lift themselves up.

O peoples, bless our God;
let the voice of God's praise resound,

of the God who gave life to our souls
and kept our feet from stumbling.

Glory be . . .

Reading Tobit 4:16, 18-19a

Give your bread to those who are hungry, and your
clothes to those who lack clothing. Of whatever you own
in plenty, devote a proportion to almsgiving; and when
you give alms, do it ungrudgingly.

Ask advice of every wise person; never scorn any
profitable advice. Bless the Lord God in everything; beg
him to guide your ways and bring your paths and
purposes to their end.

Canticle with Gospel antiphon

If anyone wants to be a follower of mine, let him
renounce himself and take up his cross and follow me.
(Mark 8:34)

Benedictus (p. 10)

Intercessions

Lord, with the dawning of a new day
we celebrate our faith in the Resurrection;
may it give us hope.
– Lord, bless your people.

Be with those who have unpleasant tasks to do today
and with those who are anxious about their work.
– Lord, bless your people.

Be with those who are suffering today
in mind or body.
– Lord, bless your people.

(Personal intercessions may be added here.)

Our Father . . .

Prayer

Lord, be the beginning and end
of all that we do and say.
Prompt our actions with your grace,
and complete them with your all-powerful help.
We make our prayer through Christ our Lord. Amen.
(Morning Prayer, Monday, Week 1)

Let us bless the Lord.
Thanks be to God.

O God, come to our aid.
O Lord, make haste to help us.
Glory be . . .

Psalm 21 (22):2-12

My God, my God, why have you forsaken me?
You are far from my plea and the cry of my distress.
O my God, I call by day and you give no reply;
I call by night and I find no peace.

Yet you, O God, are holy,
enthroned on the praises of Israel.
In you our forebears put their trust;
they trusted and you set them free.
When they cried to you, they escaped.
In you they trusted and never in vain.

But I am a worm and no man,
the butt of all, laughing-stock of the people.
All who see me deride me.
They curl their lips, they toss their heads.
'He trusted in the Lord, let him save him,
and release him if this is his friend.'

Yes, it was you who took me from the womb,
entrusted me to my mother's breast.
To you I was committed from my birth,

from my mother's womb you have been my God.
Do not leave me alone in my distress;
Come close, there is none else to help.

Glory be . . .

Reading Ephesians 4:11-13

And to some, his 'gift' was that they should be apostles;
to some prophets; to some, evangelists; to some, pastors
and teachers, to knit God's holy people together for the
work of service to build up the Body of Christ, until we all
reach unity in faith and knowledge of the Son of God and
form the perfect Man fully mature with the fullness of
Christ himself.

Canticle with Gospel antiphon

If anyone wants to be a follower of mine, let him
renounce himself and take up his cross and follow me.
(Mark 8:34)

Magnificat (p. 11)

Intercessions

Comfort those who are lonely tonight,
those who are abandoned and those in despair.
– Be with us, Lord, this night.

As we sleep this night,
others will be working for our benefit;
sustain them in their labour.
– Be with us, Lord, this night.

Strengthen our faith
that we may be faithful
in hearing and living your Word.
– Be with us, Lord, this night.

(Personal intercessions may be added here.)

Our Father . . .

Prayer

Let our worship give you glory, Lord,
who for our salvation looked upon
the lowliness of Mary your handmaid:
raise us up to share with her
the fullness of redemption.
We make our prayer through Christ our Lord. Amen.

(Evening Prayer, Monday, Week 1)

Let us bless the Lord.
Thanks be to God.

O Lord, open our lips, and
our mouth shall proclaim your praise.
Glory be . . .

Psalm 100 (101)

My song is of mercy and justice;
I sing to you, O Lord.
I will walk in the way of perfection.
O when, Lord, will you come?

I will walk with blameless heart
within my house;
I will not set before my eyes
whatever is base.

I will hate the ways of the crooked;
they shall not be my friends.
The false-hearted must keep far away;
the wicked I disown.

Those who secretly slander their neighbours
I will bring to silence.
Those of proud look and haughty heart
I will never endure.

I look to the faithful in the land
that they may dwell with me.
Those who walk in the way of perfection
shall be my friends.

No one who practises deceit
shall live within my house.
No one who utters lies shall stand
before my eyes.

Morning by morning I will silence
all the wicked in the land,
uprooting from the city of the Lord
all who do evil.

Glory be . . .

Reading 1 Corinthians 6:19-20

Do you not realise that your body is the temple of the
Holy Spirit, who is in you and whom you received from
God? You are not your own property, then; you have been
bought at a price. So use your body for the glory of God.

Canticle with Gospel antiphon

If you love me you will keep my commandments. I shall
ask the Father, and he will give you another Paraclete to
be with you for ever, the Spirit of truth. (John 14:15-16)

Benedictus (p. 10)

Intercessions

Lord, may we come to be more aware
of your presence among us

and to respect, in love,
the creation you have given us.
– Lord, open our hearts to your love.

Christ is the Light of the world;
may that light be our guide
through the dark moments of the day.
– Lord, open our hearts to your love.

Lord, may we be generous of heart
to those we meet today.
– Lord, open our hearts to your love.

(Personal intercessions may be added here.)

Our Father . . .

Prayer

Look with favour on our morning prayer, Lord,
and in your saving love
let your light penetrate the hidden places of our hearts.
May no sordid desires darken our minds,
renewed and enlightened as we are by your heavenly
grace.
We make our prayer through Christ our Lord. Amen.
(Morning Prayer, Tuesday, Week 1)

Let us bless the Lord.
Thanks be to God.

O God, come to our aid.
O Lord, make haste to help us.
Glory be . . .

Psalm 21 (22):23-27

I will tell of your name to my people
and praise you where they are assembled.
'You who fear the Lord give praise;
all children of Jacob, give glory.
Revere God, children of Israel.

For God has never despised
nor scorned the poverty of the poor,
nor looked away from them,
but has heard the poor when they cried.'

You are my praise in the great assembly.
My vows I will pay before those who fear God.
The poor shall eat and have their fill.
Those who seek the Lord shall praise the Lord.
May their hearts live for ever and ever!

Glory be . . .

Reading 1 Timothy 2:1-5

I urge then, first of all that petitions, prayers, intercessions
and thanksgiving should be offered for everyone, for

kings and others in authority, so that we may be able to live peaceful and quiet lives with all devotion and propriety. To do this is right, and acceptable to God our Saviour: he wants everyone to be saved and reach full knowledge of the truth. For there is only one God, and there is only one mediator between God and humanity, himself a human being, Christ Jesus who offered himself as a ransom for all.

Canticle with Gospel antiphon

If you love me you will keep my commandments. I shall ask the Father, and he will give you another Paraclete to be with you for ever, the Spirit of truth. (John 14:15-16)

Magnificat (p. 11)

Intercessions

Keep your Church faithful in proclaiming
your message of forgiveness, hope and love.
– Lord Jesus, you are our peace.

Comfort and strengthen those who have received
sad or troubling news today.
– Lord Jesus, you are our peace.

Be with all those throughout the world
who are united this evening
in praying in Christ's name.
– Lord Jesus, you are our peace.

(Personal intercessions may be added here.)

Our Father . . .

Prayer

We give you thanks, Lord God Almighty,
for bringing us safely to the evening of this day;
we humbly ask that the prayer we make with uplifted
    hands
may be an offering pleasing in your sight.
We make this prayer through Christ our Lord. Amen.

(Evening Prayer, Tuesday, Week 1)

Let us bless the Lord.
Thanks be to God.

O Lord, open our lips,
and our mouth shall proclaim your praise.
Glory be . . .

Psalm 94 (95)

Come ring out our joy to the Lord;
hail the rock who saves us.
Let us come before God, giving thanks,
with songs let us hail the Lord.

A mighty God is the Lord,
a great king above all gods,
in whose hands are the depths of the earth;
the heights of the mountains as well.
The sea belongs to God, who made it
and the dry land shaped by his hands.

Come in; let us bow and bend low;
let us kneel before the God who made us
for this is our God and we
the people who belong to his pasture,
the flock that is led by his hand.

O that today you would listen to God's voice!
'Harden not your hearts as at Meribah,
as on that day at Massah in the desert
when your ancestors put me to the test;
when they tried me, though they saw my work.

For forty years I was wearied of these people
and I said: "Their hearts are astray,
these people do not know my ways."
Then I took an oath in my anger:
"Never shall they enter my rest."'

Glory be . . .

Reading Colossians 1:9b-11

We ask that through perfect wisdom and spiritual
understanding you should reach the fullest knowledge of
his will and so be able to lead a life worthy of the Lord,
a life acceptable to him in all its aspects, bearing fruit
in every kind of good work and growing in knowledge
of God.

Canticle with Gospel antiphon

The kingdom of heaven is like a merchant looking for fine
pearls; when he finds one of great value he goes and sells
everything he owns and buys it. (Matthew 13:45-46)

Benedictus (p. 10)

Intercessions

You have renewed us in baptism;
renew us again today in your love.
– Lord, we trust in you.

Strengthen those, Lord,
who are in need of our prayers this morning,
especially those unable to care for themselves.
– Lord, we trust in you.

May we bring joy and hope,
not sorrow or pain,
to those we meet today.
– Lord, we trust in you.

(Personal intercessions may be added here.)

Our Father . . .

Prayer

God our Saviour.
through the grace of baptism
you made us children of light.
Hear our prayer that we may always walk in that light
and work for truth as your witnesses.
We make this prayer through Christ our Lord. Amen.

(Morning Prayer, Wednesday, Week 1)

Let us bless the Lord.
Thanks be to God.

O God, come to our aid.
O Lord, make haste to help us.
Glory be . . .

Psalm 33 (34):1-15

I will bless the Lord at all times,
God's praise is always on my lips;
in the Lord my soul shall make its boast.
The humble shall hear and be glad.

Glorify the Lord with me.
Together let us praise God's name.
I sought the Lord and was heard;
from all my terrors set free.

Look towards God and be radiant;
let your faces not be abashed.
When the poor cry out the Lord hears them
and rescues them from all their distress.

The angel of the Lord is encamped
around those who fear God, to rescue them.
Taste and see that the Lord is good.
They are happy who seek refuge in God.

Revere the Lord, you saints.
They lack nothing, who revere the Lord.

Strong lions suffer want and go hungry
but those who seek the Lord lack no blessing.

Come, children, and hear me
that I may teach you the fear of the Lord.
Who are those who long for life
and many days, to enjoy their prosperity?

Then keep your tongue from evil
and your lips from speaking deceit.
Turn aside from evil and do good;
seek and strive after peace.

Glory be . . .

Reading Romans 14:7-9

For none of us lives for himself and none of us dies for himself; while we are alive, we are living for the Lord, and when we die, we die for the Lord: and so, alive or dead, we belong to the Lord. It was for this purpose that Christ both died and came to life again: so that he might be Lord of both the dead and the living.

Canticle with Gospel antiphon

The kingdom of heaven is like a merchant looking for fine pearls; when he finds one of great value he goes and sells everything he owns and buys it. (Matthew 13:45-46)

Magnificat (p. 11)

Intercessions

We pray for Christian families;
may they be strengthened in their witness of faith.
– Bless your people, Lord.

We give thanks for the nourishment you give us
and pray for the relief of hunger and poverty.
– Bless your people, Lord.

Give rest to those who have died today;
welcome them into your peace.
– Bless your people, Lord.

(Personal intercessions may be added here.)

Our Father ...

Prayer

Lord, support us as we pray,
protect us day and night,
so that we who under your guiding hand
live in a world of change,
may always draw strength from you,
with whom there is no shadow of alteration.
We make our prayer through Christ our Lord. Amen.

(Evening Prayer, Wednesday, Week 1)

Let us bless the Lord.
Thanks be to God.

O Lord, open our lips,
and our mouth shall proclaim your praise.
Glory be . . .

Psalm 145 (146)

My soul, give praise to the Lord;
I will praise the Lord all my days,
make music to my God while I live.

Put no trust in the powerful,
mere mortals in whom there is no help.
Take their breath, they return to clay
and their plans that day come to nothing.

They are happy who are helped by Jacob's God,
whose hope is in the Lord their God,
who alone made heaven and earth,
the seas and all they contain.

It is the Lord who keeps faith for ever,
who is just to those who are oppressed.
It is God who gives bread to the hungry,
the Lord, who sets prisoners free,

the Lord who gives sight to the blind,
who raises up those who are bowed down,
the Lord, who protects the stranger
and upholds the widow and orphan.

It is the Lord who loves the just
but thwarts the path of the wicked.
The Lord will reign for ever,
Zion's God, from age to age.

Alleluia!

Glory be . . .

Reading Philippians 2:14-16a

Let your behaviour be free of murmuring and
complaining so that you remain faultless and pure,
unspoilt children of God surrounded by a deceitful and
underhand brood, shining out among them like bright
stars in the world, proffering it to the Word of life.

Canticle with Gospel antiphon

And when you stand in prayer, forgive whatever you
have against anybody, so that your Father in heaven may
forgive your failings too. (Mark 11:25)

Benedictus (p. 10)

Intercessions

As we take up again the burden of a new day,
through our sufferings may we come to see and support
the greater sufferings of others.
– Send us your Holy Spirit.

May we be united in our prayer
with all those throughout the world
who are also praying to you at this moment.
– Send us your Holy Spirit.

Deepen our spirit of prayer and praise, Lord,
and may we always give you thanks for your gifts.
– Send us your Holy Spirit.

(Personal intercessions may be added here.)

Our Father . . .

Prayer

Almighty ever-living God,
we make our prayer to you at morning, noon and evening:
dispel from our hearts the darkness of sin,
and bring us to the true light, Christ your Son,
who lives and reigns with you and the Holy Spirit,
God, for ever and ever. Amen.

(Morning Prayer, Thursday, Week 1)

Let us bless the Lord.
Thanks be to God.

O God, come to our aid.
O Lord, make haste to help us.
Glory be. . .

Psalm 22 (23)

Lord you are my shepherd
there is nothing I shall want.
Fresh and green are the pastures
where you give me repose.
Near restful waters you lead me,
to revive my drooping spirit.

You guide me along the right path;
you are true to your name.
If I should walk in the valley of darkness
no evil would I fear.
You are there with your crook and your staff;
with these you give me comfort.

You have prepared a banquet for me
in the sight of my foes.
My head you have anointed with oil;
my cup is overflowing.

Surely goodness and kindness shall follow me
all the days of my life.

In the Lord's own house shall I dwell
for ever and ever.

Glory be . . .

Reading James 5:13-16

Any one of you who is in trouble should pray; anyone in good spirits should sing a psalm. Any one of you who is ill should send for the elders of the church, and they must anoint the sick person with oil in the name of the Lord and pray over him. The prayer of faith will save the sick person and the Lord will raise him up again; and if he has committed any sins, he will be forgiven. So confess your sins to one another, and pray for one another to be cured; the heartfelt prayer of someone upright works very powerfully.

Canticle with Gospel antiphon

And when you stand in prayer, forgive whatever you have against anybody, so that your Father in heaven may forgive your failings too. (Mark 11:25)

Magnificat (p. 11)

Intercessions

Show your love, Lord,
to our families and our friends;
keep them in your care.
– Lord Jesus, you are our hope.

We pray for those who are suffering in pain tonight
and for those who have today received
bad news about their health.
– Lord Jesus, you are our hope.

We thank you for all the benefits you give us;
help us to use them wisely.
– Lord Jesus, you are our hope.

(Personal intercessions may be added here.)

Our Father . . .

Prayer

Lord God,
you give the moon to illumine the night,
and to dispel the darkness you bring in the light of day:
grant that during this night
we may elude the grasp of Satan
and in the morning rise to give you praise.
We make this prayer through Christ our Lord. Amen.

(Evening Prayer, Thursday, Week 1)

Let us bless the Lord.
Thanks be to God.

O Lord, open our lips,
and our mouth shall proclaim your praise.
Glory be. . .

Psalm 3

How many are my foes, O Lord!
How many are rising up against me!
How many are saying about me:
'No help will come from God.'

But you, Lord, are a shield about me,
my glory, who lift up my head.
I cry aloud to you, Lord.
You answer from your holy mountain.

I lie down to rest and I sleep.
I wake, for you uphold me.
I will not fear even thousands of people
who are ranged on every side against me.

Arise, Lord; save me, my God,
you who strike all my foes on the mouth,
you who break the teeth of the wicked!
O Lord of salvation, bless your people!

Glory be . . .

Reading Ephesians 2:19-22

So you are no longer aliens or foreign visitors; you are fellow-citizens with the holy people of God and part of God's household. You are built upon the foundations of the apostles and prophets, and Christ Jesus himself is the cornerstone. Every structure knit together in him grows into a holy temple in the Lord; and you too, in him, are being built up into a dwelling-place of God in the Spirit.

Canticle with Gospel antiphon

You believe because you can see me. Blessed are those who have not seen and yet believe. (John 20:29)

Benedictus (p. 10)

Intercessions

May the sacrifices we may have to make today
be made holy by the life-giving sacrifice of Christ.
– Lord Jesus, work in us today.

Help us to see the needs of our neighbours
and give us the compassion to love them.
– Lord Jesus, work in us today.

May those who design and build our cities and towns,
and those who manage our environment
always be mindful in their work

of the dignity of each human being.
– Lord Jesus, work in us today.

(Personal intercessions may be added here.)

Our Father . . .

Prayer

Lord God,
you hold out the light of your Word
to those who do not know you.
Strengthen in our hearts the faith you have given us,
so that no trials may quench the fire
your Spirit has kindled within us.
We make this prayer through Christ our Lord. Amen.

(Morning Prayer, Friday, Week 1)

Let us bless the Lord.
Thanks be to God.

O God, come to our aid.
O Lord, make haste to help us.
Glory be. . .

Psalm 51 (52)

Why do you boast of your wickedness,
you champion of evil,
planning ruin all day long,
(your tongue like a sharpened razor),
you dealer in deceit?

You love evil more than good,
lies more than truth.
You love the destructive word,
you tongue of deceit.

For this God will destroy you
and remove you for ever.
God will snatch you from your tent and uproot you
from the land of the living.

The just shall see and fear.
They shall laugh and say:
'So this is the one who refused
to take God as a stronghold,
but trusted in the power of wealth
and grew powerful through crime.'

But I am like a growing olive tree
in the house of God.
I trust in the goodness of God
for ever and ever.

I will thank you for evermore;
for this is your doing.
I will proclaim that your name is good,
in the presence of your friends.

Glory be . . .

Reading 1 Peter 1:6-8

This is a great joy to you, even though for a short time yet
you must bear all sorts of trials; so that the worth of your
faith, more valuable than gold, which is perishable even if
it has been tested by fire, may be proved – to your praise
and honour when Jesus Christ is revealed. You have not
seen him, yet you love him; and still without seeing him
you believe in him and so are already filled with a joy so
glorious that it cannot be described.

Canticle with Gospel antiphon

You believe because you can see me. Blessed are those
who have not seen and yet believe. (John 20:29)

Magnificat (p. 11)

185

Intercessions

Comfort those who today have lost a loved one.
Receive the dead into your kingdom.
– Lord, show us your mercy.

Move us to reach out in love
to those rejected by the world
and by themselves.
– Lord, show us your mercy.

We give thanks for the joy of our Christian faith;
strengthen those whose faith causes them difficulties.
– Lord, show us your mercy.

(Personal intercessions may be added here.)

Our Father . . .

Prayer

Lord God,
teach us the lessons of your Son's Passion,
and so enable us, your people,
to bear the yoke he makes light for us.
We make this prayer through Christ our Lord. Amen.
(Evening Prayer, Friday, Week 1)

Let us bless the Lord.
Thanks be to God.

O Lord, open our lips,
and our mouth shall proclaim your praise.
Glory be . . .

Psalm 99 (100)

Cry out with joy to the Lord, all the earth.
Serve the Lord with gladness.
Come before God, singing for joy.

Know that the Lord is God,
our Maker, to whom we belong.
We are God's people, sheep of the flock.

Enter the gates with thanksgiving,
God's courts with songs of praise.
Give thanks to God and bless his name.

Indeed, how good is the Lord,
whose merciful love is eternal;
whose faithfulness lasts forever.

Glory be . . .

Reading Colossians 3:16-17

Let the Word of Christ, in all its richness, find a home with
you. Teach each other, and advise each other, in all wisdom.

With gratitude in your hearts sing psalms and hymns and inspired songs to God; and whatever you say or do, let it be in the name of the Lord Jesus, in thanksgiving to God the Father through him.

Canticle with Gospel antiphon

It is not anyone who says to me, 'Lord, Lord,' who will enter the kingdom of heaven, but the person who does the will of my Father in heaven. (Matthew 7:21)

Benedictus (p. 10)

Intercessions

Our faith in you lightens our path for the coming day;
we pray for those who have no faith
to guide and comfort them.
– Lord, show us your love.

Lord, teach us to see you
in all our brothers and sisters.
– Lord, show us your love.

Inspire those who are creative in art, music and word
to reflect your glory
and to bring joy and understanding into our lives.
– Lord, show us your love.

(Personal intercessions may be added here.)

Our Father . . .

Prayer

Almighty Lord and God,
protect us by your power throughout the course of this day,
even as you have enabled us to begin it:
do not let us turn aside to any sin,
but let our every thought, word and deed
aim at doing what is pleasing in your sight.
We make this prayer through Christ our Lord. Amen.
(Morning Prayer, Monday, Week 2)

Let us bless the Lord.
Thanks be to God.

Evening Prayer

O God, come to our aid.
O Lord, make haste to help us.
Glory be . . .

Psalm 12 (13)

How long, O Lord, will you forget me?
How long will you hide your face?
How long must I bear grief in my soul,
this sorrow in my heart day and night?
How long shall my enemy prevail?

Look at me, answer me, Lord my God!
Give light to my eyes lest I fall asleep in death,
lest my enemy say: 'I have prevailed';
lest my foes rejoice to see my fall.

As for me, I trust in your merciful love.
Let my heart rejoice in your saving help.
Let me sing to you Lord for your goodness to me,
sing psalms to your name, O Lord, Most High.

Glory be . . .

Reading 1 John 2:3-6

In this way we know that we have come to know him, if
we keep his commandments. Whoever says, 'I know him,

without keeping his commandments, is a liar, and truth has no place in him. But anyone who does keep his word, in such a one God's love truly reaches its perfection. This is the proof that we are in God. Whoever claims to remain in such a person must act as he acted.

Canticle with Gospel antiphon

It is not anyone who says to me, 'Lord, Lord,' who will enter the kingdom of heaven, but the person who does the will of my Father in heaven. (Matthew 7:21)

Magnificat (p. 11)

Intercessions

Give us the rest we need,
that we may be ever more eager to do your will.
– Lord, give us your protection.

Guide the leaders of your Church
that they may be instruments of your love and peace.
– Lord, give us your protection.

Be with those who are suffering tonight
and comfort those who are in distress.
– Lord, give us your protection.

(Personal intercessions may be added here.)

Our Father . . .

Prayer

All-powerful God,
since you have given us, your unworthy servants,
the strength to work throughout this day:
accept this evening sacrifice of praise
as we thank you for your gifts.
We make this prayer through Christ our Lord. Amen.

(Evening Prayer, Monday, Week 2)

Let us bless the Lord.
Thanks be to God.

Morning Prayer

O Lord, open our lips,
and our mouth shall proclaim your praise.
Glory be . . .

Psalm 56 (57):2-4, 8-12

Have mercy on me, God, have mercy
for in you my soul has taken refuge.
In the shadow of your wings I take refuge
till the storms of destruction pass by.

I call to you God the Most High,
to you who have always been my help.
May you send from heaven and save me
and shame those who assail me.

O God, send your truth and your love.

My heart is ready, O God,
my heart is ready.
I will sing, I will sing your praise.
Awake my soul;
awake, lyre and harp,
I will awake the dawn.

I will thank you, Lord, among the peoples,
among the nations I will praise you
for your love reaches to the heavens
and your truth to the skies.

O God, arise above the heavens;
may your glory shine on earth!

Glory be . . .

Reading Philippians 2:1-5a

So if in Christ there is anything that will move you, any incentive in love, any fellowship in the Spirit, any warmth or sympathy – I appeal to you, make my joy complete by being of a single mind, one in love, one in heart and one in mind. Nothing is done out of jealousy or vanity; instead, out of humility of mind everyone should give preference to others, everyone pursuing not selfish interests but those of others. Make your own the mind of Christ Jesus.

Canticle with Gospel antiphon

The disciples were filled with joy at seeing the Lord, and he said to them again, 'Peace be with you. As the Father sent me, so am I sending you'. (John 20:21)

Benedictus (p. 10)

Intercessions

Lord, may we come to be more aware
of your presence among us
and to respect, in love, the creation you have given us.
– Lord, open our hearts to your love.

Christ is the Light of the world;
may that light be our guide
through the dark moments of the day.
– Lord, open our hearts to your love.

Lord, may we be generous of heart
to those we meet today.
– Lord, open our hearts to your love.

(Personal intercessions may be added here.)

Our Father . . .

Prayer

True Light of the world, Lord Jesus Christ,
as you enlighten all men and women for their salvation,
give us grace, we pray,
to herald your coming
by preparing the ways of justice and of peace.
Who live and reign with the Father and the Holy Spirit,
God, for ever and ever. Amen.

(Morning Prayer, Tuesday, Week 2)

Let us bless the Lord.
Thanks be to God.

Evening Prayer

O God, come to our aid.
O Lord, make haste to help us.
Glory be . . .

Psalm 110 (111)

I will thank the Lord with all my heart
in the meeting of the just and their assembly.
Great are the works of the Lord,
to be pondered by all who love them.

Majestic and glorious God's work,
whose justice stands firm for ever.
God makes us remember these wonders.
The Lord is compassion and love.

God gives food to those who fear him;
keeps his covenant ever in mind;
shows mighty works to his people
by giving them the land of the nations.

God's works are justice and truth,
God's precepts are all of them sure,
standing firm for ever and ever;
they are made in uprightness and truth.

God has sent deliverance to his people
and established his covenant for ever.
Holy is God's name, to be feared.

To fear the Lord is the first stage of wisdom;
all who do so prove themselves wise.
God's praise shall last for ever!

Glory be . . .

Reading Colossians 1:3-6a

We give thanks for you to God, the Father of our Lord
Jesus Christ, continually in our prayers, ever since we
heard about your faith in Christ Jesus and the love that
you show towards all God's holy people because of the
hope which is stored up for you in heaven. News of this
hope reached you not long ago through the word of truth,
the Gospel that came to you in the same way as it is
bearing fruit and growing throughout the world.

Canticle with Gospel antiphon

The disciples were filled with joy at seeing the Lord, and
he said to them again, 'Peace be with you. As the Father
sent me, so am I sending you.' (John 20:21)

Magnificat (p. 11)

Intercessions

Keep your Church faithful in proclaiming
your message of forgiveness, hope and love.
– Lord Jesus, you are our peace.

Comfort and strengthen those
who have received sad or troubling news today.
– Lord Jesus, you are our peace.

Be with all those throughout the world
who are united this evening in praying in Christ's name.
– Lord Jesus, you are our peace.

(Personal intercessions may be added here.)

Our Father . . .

Prayer

Yours is the day and yours the night, Lord God:
let the Sun of Justice shine so steadily in our hearts,
that we may come at length
to that light where you dwell eternally.
We make this prayer through Christ our Lord. Amen.
(Evening Prayer, Tuesday, Week 2)

Let us bless the Lord.
Thanks be to God.

NIGHT PRAYER (Compline)

O God, come to our aid.
O Lord, make haste to help us.
Glory be . . .

*Take a few moments to think over the past day, thanking God
for successes and blessings and acknowledging as one's own,
failures, faults and opportunities missed.*

The following, or some similar petitions, are said:

Lord, we have sinned against you;
Lord, have mercy.

Lord, show us your mercy and love.
And grant us your salvation.

May Almighty God have mercy on us,
forgive us our sins
and bring us to everlasting life. Amen.

*The three traditional Compline Psalms are given. All three psalms
may be said or one selected.*

Psalm 4

When I call, answer me, O God of justice;
from anguish you released me, have mercy and hear me!

You rebels, how long will your hearts be closed,
will you love what is futile and seek what is false?

It is the Lord who grants favour to those who are
    merciful;
the Lord who hears me whenever I call.

Tremble; do not sin: ponder on your bed and be still.
Make justice your sacrifice and trust in the Lord.

'What can bring us happiness?' many say.
Lift up the light of your face on us, O Lord.

You have put into my heart a greater joy
than they have from abundance of corn and new wine.

I will lie down in peace and sleep comes at once
for you alone, Lord, make me dwell in safety.

Glory be . . .

Psalm 90 (91)

Those who dwell in the shelter of the Most High
and abide in the shade of the Almighty
say to the Lord: 'My refuge,
my stronghold, my God in whom I trust!'

It is God who will free you from the snare
of the fowler who seeks to destroy you;
God will conceal you with his pinions,
and under his wings you will find refuge.

You will not fear the terror of the night
nor the arrow that flies by day,
nor the plague that prowls in the darkness
nor the scourge that lays waste at noon.

A thousand may fall at your side,
ten thousand fall at your right,
you, it will never approach;
God's faithfulness is buckler and shield.

Your eyes have only to look
to see how the wicked are repaid,
you who have said: 'Lord, my refuge!'
and have made the Most High your dwelling.

Upon you no evil shall fall,
no plague approach where you dwell.
For you God has commanded the angels,
to keep you in all your ways.

They shall bear you upon their hands
lest you strike your foot against a stone.
On the lion and the viper you will tread
and trample the young lion and the dragon.

You set your love on me so I will save you,
protect you for you know my name.
When you call I shall answer: 'I am with you,'
I will save you in distress and give you glory.

With length of days I will content you;
I shall let you see my saving power.

Glory be . . .

Psalm 133 (134)

O come, bless the Lord,
all you who serve the Lord,
who stand in the house of the Lord,
in the courts of the house of our God.

Lift up your hands to the holy place
and bless the Lord through the night.

May the Lord bless you from Zion,
God who made both heaven and earth.

Glory be . . .

Reading 1 Thessalonians 5:23

May the God of peace make you perfect and holy; and
may your spirit, life and body be kept blameless for the
coming of our Lord Jesus Christ.

Responsory

R. Into your hands, O Lord, I commend my spirit.
V. You have redeemed us, Lord God of truth.
R. Into your hands, O Lord, I commend my spirit.
V. Glory be to the Father and to the Son, and to the Holy
Spirit.
R. Into your hands, O Lord, I commend my spirit.

Gospel Canticle with antiphon

(Said before and after the Nunc Dimittis.)

Save us, Lord, while we are awake; protect us while we sleep; that we may keep watch with Christ and rest with him in peace.

Nunc Dimittis (Luke 2:29-32)

At last, all-powerful Master,
you give leave to your servant
to go in peace, according to your promise.

For my eyes have seen your salvation
which you have prepared for all nations,
the light to enlighten the Gentiles
and give glory to Israel, your people.

Glory be . . .

Prayer

Visit this house, we pray you, Lord:
drive far away from it all the snares of the enemy.
May your holy angels stay here and guard us in peace,
and let your blessing be always upon us.
Through Christ our Lord. Amen.

Blessing

May the Lord grant us a quiet night and a perfect end. Amen.

Antiphon to Our Lady (Salve Regina)

Hail, Holy Queen, mother of mercy; hail, our life, our sweetness, and our hope. To you do we cry, poor banished children of Eve; to you do we send up our sighs, mourning and weeping in this vale of tears. Turn then, most gracious advocate, your eyes of mercy towards us; and after this our exile, show us the blessed fruit of your womb, Jesus. O clement, O loving, O sweet Virgin Mary.